Beyond the Dental Chair

DIDmedia
PUBLICATIONS

Beyond the Dental Chair

A Proven, Less Stressful,
More Manageable Approach
for Dental Practice Success

Gary E. Stough, DMD

ACKNOWLEDGMENTS

Having an idea and turning it into a book is as hard as it sounds. How blessed I am to have an English Major spouse, Diane, and three very educated offspring, Dr. Alexa Chilcutt, Boyd Stough esq and Laurel Stough, to review my earlier drafts and suggest many positive suggestions for improvement. No one is more aware of my background and philosophy of dental practice than they I am also grateful for the help of two of my private practice general dentistry classmates, Drs. Ed Wheeler and Isabelle Heberger and Dr. Art Jeske, Associate Dean for Strategic Planning and CE and Professor in the Department of General Practice and Dental Public Health at the University of Texas Dental School in Houston, Texas . I have never been one to think I had all the answers and saw all possibilities so the help of these dear people was invaluable and I owe each of them an extraordinary debt of thanks. I was fortunate to find an incredible young man, Mr. Jason Blaxkburn, owner of DID Media, to help me prepare the book for publication and for his invaluable advice. This effort is simply a combination of seminars and articles from my past and real life private practice experience and my hope is that some might gain a bit of helpful information to improve their practice and personal life in the future.

TABLE OF CONTENTS

INTRODUCTION

First, allow me to sincerely thank you for purchasing this book. My primary goal in writing it is to help fellow dentists experience greater practice success and significantly reduce stress, all the while prioritizing what is truly important in life professionally and personally. The idea is to make the journey from dental school graduation to retirement a more rewarding and enjoyable one. Every dentist knows that clinical skills alone are not enough for long-term success. In fact, many practitioners struggle unnecessarily by equating technical ability with fulfillment. This book is my way of giving back to a profession that has given me far more blessings than I deserve. I've distilled decades of experience into practical lessons: blending leadership, communication, business acumen and life wisdom with the raw honesty of my personal success.

Many readers feel they are doing most everything right but hopefully even they will pick up a beneficial idea or two. Lasting success requires the aforementioned skills but also the cultivation of an excellent practice perception in the community. Internal marketing in particular is an essential theme woven throughout this book and explored in depth in the following chapters. My approach to dentistry has always been based on common sense—nothing overly complex or philosophical. I am most certainly no guru, nor do I pretend to have all the answers. Rather, I am a straightforward general dentist who ran a successful practice in a small town but with plenty of nearby competition. Early in my career I recognized that if I could competently perform a wide variety of dental procedures, limit unnecessary referrals, thereby keeping more income in my own practice, consistently exceed patient expectations, keep my schedule filled with good, respectful, appreciative patients who kept appointments and paid on time, and surrounded myself with a great team, I could significantly reduce stress and retire comfortably on my own terms when I desired—financially, emotionally, and physically ready for the next chapter in life.

While many readers are already successful, likely more skilled clinicians, financially well off, and smarter individuals than myself, I believe everyone can benefit to some extent from reading this book. Let me illustrate with a personal story. In my early years in practice, working five exhausting days a week, I found myself short of CE credits needed for license renewal. I signed up for a weekend course in periodontics at the state dental school, two hours away, which did not require me to miss work and just one night's hotel stay. Money was tight. I had been performing full-mouth periodontal surgery from my first month in practice, but CE was CE.

I was initially bored and considered leaving early but stayed for the final session and learned three transformative procedures in the afternoon session. I subsequently performed those hundreds of times, greatly benefiting both my patients and my practice income. On the way home I realized how valuable the course had been because it reinforced much of what I was already doing and taught me even more. This validated an essential truth: even seemingly small insights can yield tremendous rewards.

We each have our own style of practicing dentistry. I personally am very gregarious and love interacting with people, and from the moment they walk through the office door my hope and goal is to establish a long-term trusting relationship. I surround myself with a team who feel the same as I do. Don't get me wrong. I am no pushover, make rules for patients and staff, and expect all parties to adhere to them.

If I give 100%, I expect 100% in return—for employees to do their job, patients to keep appointments, pay bills, treat my staff with respect, and cooperate, or they can seek dental care elsewhere and make another dentist's life miserable. This is seldom the case, thankfully. Others may have a different approach, and if it works for them, keep it up. Just keep in mind that a dental practice is a business first and foremost, not fun and games. The idea is to be successful, make as few bad mistakes as possible, enjoy a good living, have the respect of patients and the community at large, and retire when you want with all your mental marbles intact and a hefty bank account.

Since most dental school graduates have little or no prior experience in essential leadership, enhanced communication skills, or business acumen—skills needed in addition to clinical expertise necessary to attain a high level of practice success in the future, they begin practice life unprepared for the real world. Many dental schools have added much-needed courses in practice management, but nothing will suffice more than actually working in the trenches as a practicing dentist and learning these skills through observation, trial, and error. That is why this book stresses proven, common-sense approaches that have been effective in my journey as a private practice dentist so as to limit as much as possible unnecessary stress and pitfalls along the way.

Financial success is undeniably important, but equally critical is maintaining a balanced, fulfilling life outside the office. Maintaining family priorities and keeping physical and emotional health and mental well-being at the forefront will ensure you enjoy your career journey to the fullest. Some of the happiest dentists I know have continued practicing long after they could retire because they love it, not because they have to. Conversely, some of the unhappiest dentists continue working from necessity due to poor planning or unforeseen circumstances. Each of us holds the responsibility for our own choices and outcome. Ultimately, all we can do is strive for control and make the best possible decisions and embrace the journey. We all face pitfalls in the learning process but the goal is to learn from them and overcome them as best possible in the future.

This book is not about dentistry alone. Ultimately, what matters is not the crowns we place or accolades we earn, but the relationships we build and the lives we touch.

We each must learn to :

- Manage stress with intention

- Lead with authenticity
- Exceed expectations consistently
- Prioritize wisely
- Retire with purpose, not regret

I always love to hear from readers so feel free to contact me at Gstoughdmd@gmail.com.

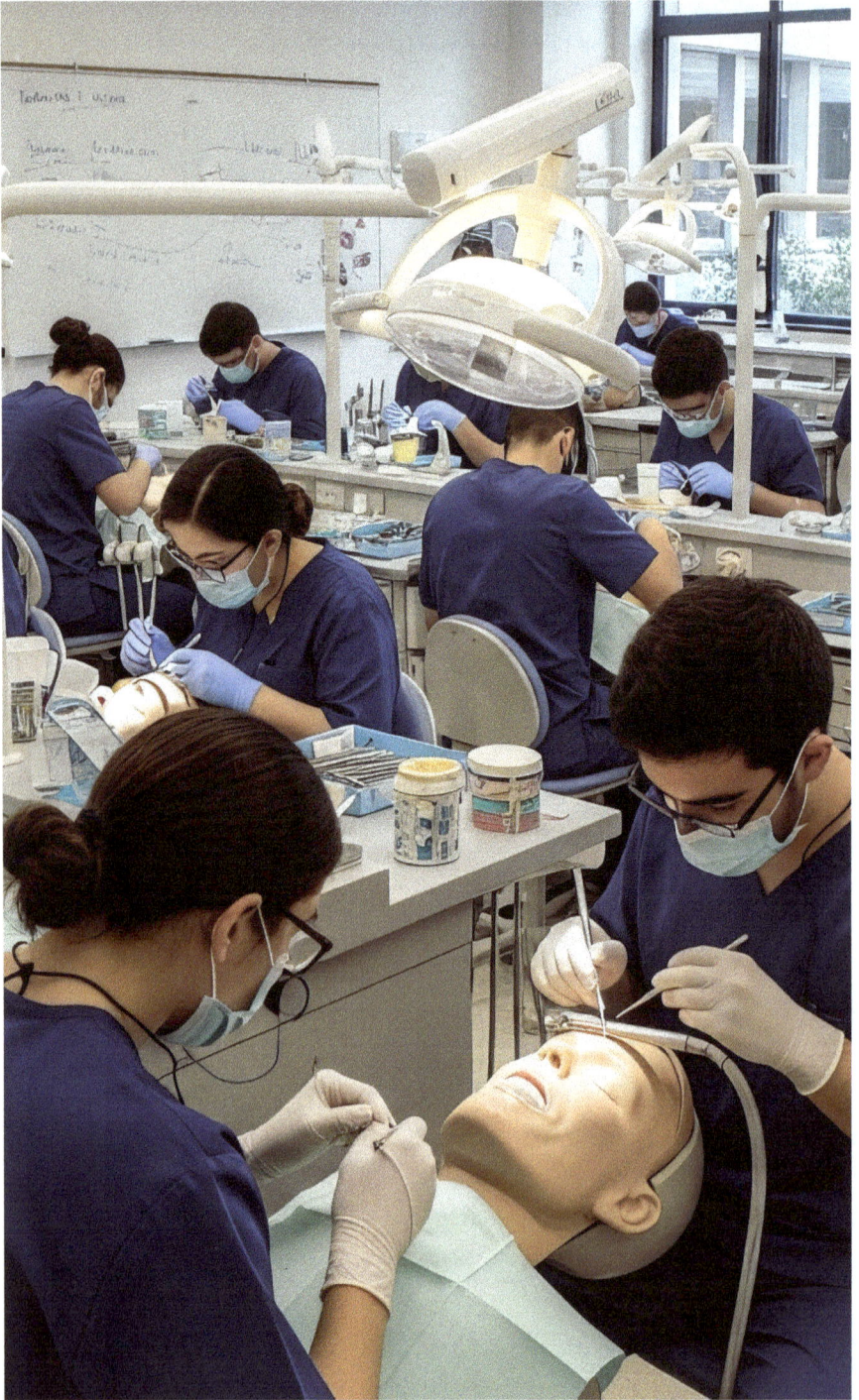

Chapter 1

DR. GARY'S "TAO"
A PERSONAL PERSPECTIVE

I was excited when granted an interview after applying to dental school at 29 years old. With a wife and young daughter and as a former Marine Corps aviator with many combat missions under my belt and a promising military career, I had left the service, gone back to school and was pursuing a different course in life. There were no guarantees and periodically I considered if I had made a mistake. But the old adage " No guts, no glory" kept me going. Having spent a good deal of time with my brother-in -law, a recent dental school graduate, I liked the idea of following in his footsteps. During the interview, when asked why I wanted to be a dentist, I gave straightforward, non-sentimental, non-flowery, and non-do-gooder reasons and simply stated I considered dentistry a well-respected, important profession that offered prospects to make a good living and give me some autonomy in directing my future. I had great hand-eye coordination, was outgoing, and communicated well with people of all ages and felt sure I could be successful.Thankfully I was accepted!

After graduation I passed up several good opportunities to join practices in large metropolitan areas and chose to start a practice in a small town in North Georgia. While there was no shortage of dentists in the area, with three established practices within a quarter mile, none did any more than basic dental procedures, and the nearest specialist was 23 miles away. In the beginning I performed full-mouth periodontal surgery, impacted third molars, and molar endo, but as my practice became extremely busy, I began referring most of these procedures to specialists but continued doing a few of the aforementioned procedures on a case-by-case basis because it made me feel like a real general dentist and was a service to both my bottom line and my patients.

I still pinch myself daily and thank the Lord for being a dentist. All that being said, dentistry has always simply been something I did, a means to an end, a job and really nothing more. Jobs and titles do not define our worth. What matters is who we are beyond the profession, the relationships we nurture and the balance we strike between ambition and peace of mind. We should not need titles or others' opinions to give us value. When I worked as a cook and dishwasher going to college the first time, it never bothered me when, on occasion, people looked down on me. I knew my job was just a means to an end to get a degree and a commission in the Marine Corps. When I no longer flew, I did not look to the sky every day and lament my decision. It was something I did and much preferable to walking through the jungle with snakes, which scare me to death, and other creatures, sleeping on the ground and eating C-rations. Flying was a means to an end to prevent such a scenario. I simply give some thought to my attitude and philosophy towards the practice of dentistry and life in general, which I feel is a healthy way to look at things. You may disagree, but I hope most readers find some positive food for thought. If we consider being a dentist who we are as a person and the primary thing that gives us a sense of worthiness, then we will experience emotional difficulty when it comes time to step away. The idea is to have something to go to, to look forward to, so that we will not always be looking back. Develop hobbies and interests, get involved in volunteer efforts, plan extensive travel, and have something to go to or look forward to outside of dentistry and enjoy the eventual transition on your own terms. Be bold and courageous because, when one looks back on their life, they will regret things they did not do more than the things they did. There are no do-overs, no Life 102, only Life 101!

The following are some concepts I hold to that I feel make the journey from dental school graduation to retirement a smoother pathway.

1. **Dentistry is a business.** Dentistry is a means to an end, not the end in itself.

2. **Cultivate the right combination of skills.** The primary keys to

practice success are good-to-excellent clinical skills, an engaging personality, communication skills, proactive leadership, personal integrity, and relationship building. One must develop a business acumen and trust in their own common sense. They should listen to others but let the final decisions be their own. Be decisive, even if it means sometimes you're wrong. More often than not, you will be right.

3. **Set yourself apart from others by caring more.** Perception is important. Have patients value you as a person as much as they value your dental skills. Always give people more than they expect.

4. **Hire only staff who have the interpersonal skills you desire.** You want patients to feel special and appreciated by everyone they come in contact with in your office setting.

5. **Start planning for retirement early.** By planning early, you can make better decisions that align with and advance your particular vision for the future.

6. **Avoid the "Big hat, no cattle" lifestyle.** Books to read: The *Book of Proverbs* in the *Old Testament*, *The Millionaire Next Door* (Thomas J. Stanley and William D. Danko), and *Who Moved My Cheese* (Spencer Johnson, MD). Refrain from trying to always keep up with others.

7. **Be a leader.** Earn the respect of your staff. Be friendly, caring, and concerned, but do not enter into close personal relationships.

8. **Avoid get-rich schemes.** Avoid these types of "opportunities" completely, or make sure everyone involved has as much to lose financially as you do. Make sure you're getting guidance from someone who has relevant expertise.

9. **Be honest!** Do unto others as you would have them do unto you. A reputation is a valuable asset and hard to regain once lost.

10. **Build and maintain a valuable network.** You may have heard the old adage "Your network is your net worth." While your network isn't entirely indicative of your character and likelihood of success, a network of reputable professionals is truly invalu-

able. Take the time to thoughtfully build relationships with other dental professionals whose character and success you would like to emulate, and remember to give back as much as (if not more than) you receive.

11. **DO NOT GET INTO A RUT.** Keep things exciting by expanding or improving clinical skills through CE. Commit yourself to quality! This includes your life away from the office.

12. **THE DOOR SWINGS BOTH WAYS.** Care for your patients, make them feel appreciated, and be there for them in their times of need, but if they fail to keep appointments, are habitually late or disrespectful to your staff, or fail to pay bills, fire them! When you commit to only working for patients that value you as much as you value them, you'll be much happier.

13. **BUILD A FIRM LIFESTYLE FOUNDATION.** Thoughtfully developing a lifestyle that balances work, family, and recreation is important to maintaining your edge (and your sanity). It's best to firm this up early, but it is never too late to change.

14. **FOCUS ON WHAT REALLY MATTERS RATHER THAN MATERIAL THINGS.** Happiness is not about your possessions, power, or status in the community but is measured by meaningful relationships and the love and respect of others. That does not mean you should limit your income level. Simply make an effort to be thankful and humble at all times and maintain perspective. Doing so will serve you well in your practice and in life.

15. **PERSISTENCE IS THE KEY.** Success has been defined as the gradual realization of a worthy ideal. Success isn't so much about outcome, although that is important, but rather the everyday experience of those who persist through and overcome adversity. If you have a vision and that vision is truly worthy of your best efforts, focused and persistent effort will give way to what some call "the compound effect," which means you'll enjoy bigger, better results with time.

Whenever giving a lecture or speaking to dental students, I always ask the question "Can someone give me a definition of WISDOM?"

As one can imagine, the answers run the gamut from Einstein, Plato, Socrates, and Solomon and beyond, but invariably someone will say "common sense." Common sense is the crux!!! I define wisdom as the awareness that each of us is an imperfect human being living in an imperfect world, and we will make mistakes. Those mistakes can affect us and define our future in a negative or positive manner. If they defeat us, ruin our confidence and self-perception, and we give up and quit trying for fear of further failure and disappointment, then we lose the opportunity. If we use those mistakes as learning tools as to what not to do in the future and make adjustments going forward, then we will come out better for the experience. Wisdom is also considering the ramifications of decisions. If a decision can negatively affect our health, finances, reputation, marriage, self-esteem, or other areas of our life, consider if it is worth doing. That does not mean never to extend ourselves or take chances but to carefully weigh positive versus negative possibilities.

"It is not the critic who counts; not the man who points out how the strong man stumbles, or where the doer of deeds could have done them better. The credit belongs to the man who is actually in the arena, whose face is marred by dust and sweat and blood; who strives valiantly; who errs, who comes short again and again, because there is no effort without error and shortcoming; but who does actually strive to do the deeds; who knows great enthusiasms, the great devotions; who spends himself in a worthy cause; who at the best knows in the end the triumph of high achievement, and who at the worst, if he fails, at least fails while daring greatly, so that his place shall never be with those cold and timid souls who neither know victory nor defeat." - Theodore Roosevelt

KEY TAKAWAYS

- Dentistry-or any profession-is a business, not a total identity
- Persistence, common sense and honesty remain the greatest tools for success
- Life's regrets more often come from things left undone, not from risks taken

REFLECTION AND PRACTICE

- Write down three aspects of your identity that have nothing to do with your profession
- What hobbies, interests or relationships could you invest in today to give your life more balance
- Ask yourself: If my career ended tomorrow, what would give me meaning going forward
- Write down one mistake that once felt like a failure but later taught you wisdom.
- Reflect: What legacy do you want to leave for yourself and your extended family- not just in work but in life?

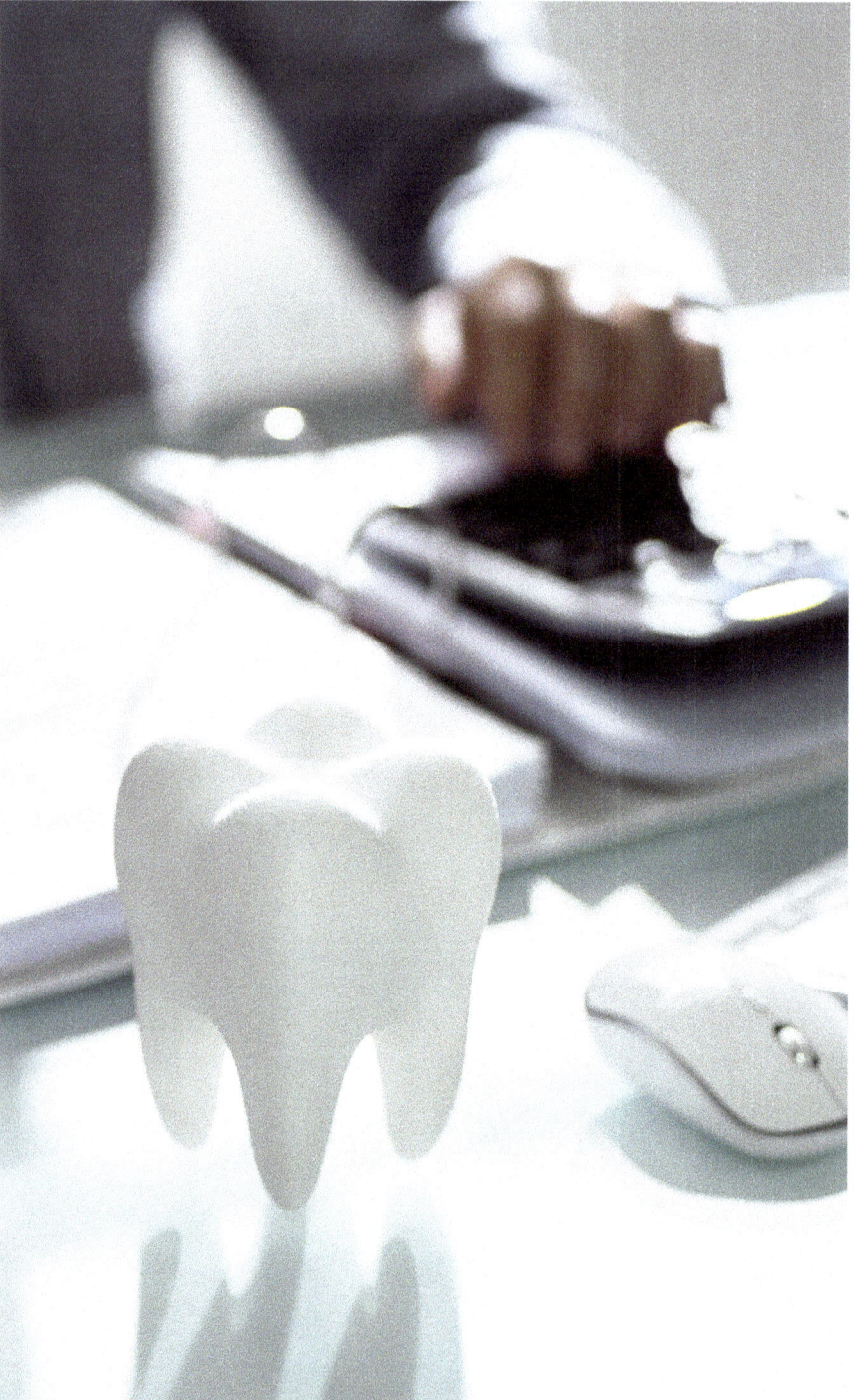

Chapter 2

DENTISTRY IS A BUSINESS

While I consider myself a good business person and capable of giving some business advice I suggest, when seeking specialized guidance, one hire a professional with expertise in the dental field, preferably a former private practice dentist. No one really knows how to run a successful dental practice unless they have been in the same fox hole sometime in their life. Managing a dental practice has some unique requirements of its own. While clinical skills are essential to dental practice success they alone are no guarantee because strong business habits are crucial for long term growth and stability in every case. They lay the foundation but it is a dedication to and passion for business mastery that transforms potential into prosperity. These include understanding financial management, effective marketing, especially internal marketing, leadership and time management. By blending clinical expertise with sound business strategies, dentists can build thriving practices that offer excellent patient care and financial success.

Importance Of Business Acumen

Too many dentists struggle, even after years in practice, acutely aware they should be doing better but having not attained the level of practice success they once hoped for at their time in their life. As stated many times throughout this book, building practice success depends on clinical expertise, effective leadership, good communication and good business strategies and any dentist lacking in any of these areas will never reach the pinnacle of success. Obviously some readers are doing it all right and are great success stories but, for those who feel they can do better, hopefully they gain some insight into improving their current practice situation.

Marketing And Patient Relationships

Effective marketing requires developing a strong online presence, leveraging social media and community outreach, but most importantly, maximizing internal marketing as discussed in the chapters PRACTICE PERCEPTION; TIMEX OR ROLEX and EFFECTIVE INTERNAL MARKETING METHODS. Building excellent patient relations, communicating well, building trust and providing exceptional customer service encourages patient loyalty and referrals. These should be the primary goals for any business.

As a business leader it is important to foster a positive workplace culture, keeping your team motivated, exceeding expectations at all times and leading by example in order to create a cohesive, productive environment. Effective leadership is discussed in the chapter on Leadership. No business will ever succeed if there is no cohesive office atmosphere.

Time And Financial Management

Time management is so important. Good management of the schedule and prioritizing tasks ensures balance between clinical duties and business operations. Financial management requires detailed record keeping, budgeting wisely and understanding cash flow. Learn to delegate responsibly but do not leave this job solely to someone else because this is YOUR business.

My father used to say it isn't how much you make but how much you keep that is important when talking about personal finances and the same goes with a business. The average dental practice overhead is between 65% and 70% but in many cases much more. Some areas of expense, like payroll, employee compensation, facility costs and administration expenses are fairly fixed in most cases while lab costs, dental equipment and supplies vary. Money spent for equipment and supplies and lab costs are areas we have more control over reducing expenditures. Periodically examine and make adjustments as needed. Many dentists have a tendency to purchase expensive equipment for ego that is seldom used or will be a long term payment expense or they pay up front with funds that may have been better utilized elsewhere. A dentist should always evaluate the pros and cons of equipment purchases and the potential benefits to their personal practice circumstances. I personally could never make sense of purchasing an expensive CEREC machine. We do our share of crown and bridge work but that is not our main area of focus. We more than make up income by offering a wide variety of other clinical procedures which are a service to our patients and keep the money in our practice rather than someone else's. Initially lasers had limitations and I refused to have it sitting in a closet and seldom used but lasers have improved greatly and may be a wise investment for some practices. If a dentist can justify any expense when evaluating their own office needs and make maximum use of them, then obviously the expense is worth it. It is important to keep up with technology and materials and to stay competitive and a dentist should never hesitate to spend the money if they see the benefits to their practice but also make maximum use of what you already have. Chairside digital radiography, Intra-oral cameras, Pan x ray units and x-ray units in each operatory enhance patient education, efficiency and profitability. Intraoral scanners, CAD/CAM systems including 3D printing and A-I powered diagnostic tools are wise investments in most cases. That being said, always make maximum, most effective usage of equipment before discarding for the next. Three of my six dental chairs are the initial Pelton Crane chairs I purchased when starting my practice. They look brand new because I have had them beautifully recovered twice. Much less expensive than purchasing new chairs and they are still beautiful. I would rather be referred to as frugal than cheap!!!!.

Controlling Overhead

One must consider the variables in facility costs because rents and mortgage payments vary greatly and can eat up a good chunk of monthly income. In my case, I built a brick duplex office using one side for my practice and renting out the other side and was able to pay the building off in 10 years which greatly reduced my overhead going forward. Purchasing or renting is a big decision. If a practice is in a dense metropolitan area then it may be out of the question economically to build or purchase and renting seems prudent. In suburban, small towns or more rural areas it makes a lot more sense so I suggest examining the financial numbers long term and decide what works best for you for the future. If currently renting, owning your office building builds equity for the future and can enhance retirement financial security.

If a practice grosses $1 million a year but has 75% overhead the dentist(s) makes $250,000 before taxes. Reducing the overhead 5% results in an additional $50,000 yearly net profit. Another way to reduce overhead is to keep monthly costs fixed while increasing income and that can be done by reducing and almost eliminating holes in the schedule and being aggressive with accounts receivables. We discuss this more in the chapter on effective scheduling. Dentists often are hesitant to raise prices, especially in highly competitive markets which I certainly understand, but it is something that must be done on a yearly basis just to keep up with cost and inflation.

The increases do not have to be big. Even a 3%-5% increase can be beneficial and the patient seldom notices. If it is a concern, patients notice more on the big procedures such as crown and bridge, but less on areas like cleanings, composites and extractions so you might wish to concentrate more on those areas.

Schedule Control

Managing the schedule is critical which we discuss at length in the chapter entitled CONTROLLING THE SCHEDULE. Financial loss from unfilled chair time quickly adds up. Five hours of weekly down time can cost the practice thousands annually. Calculate the hourly production of your practice and the lost revenue from open schedule slots and the numbers are eye opening and should motivate any dentist to make every effort to maintain a consistently full schedule. Establishing rules and demanding patients adhere to them and dismissing uncooperative patients, having a well structured call list and other suggestions in that chapter can increase income significantly. If you average $250 an hour production and have 5 hours of open schedule time a week in a four day work week, the annual loss of income is $60,000. A practice grossing a million dollars a year averages $652 hourly in production. Five hours of open schedule time equates to a yearly loss of over $150,000. In either scenario it is an issue to be seriously dealt with. By setting rules beforehand, dismissing uncooperative patients thereby letting other patients know you mean business, having a team member have access to the schedule at night to confirm and fill any open time (lab cases are a pretty sure fill- in) and managing the call list effectively an office can keep the schedule filled and benefit from the financial rewards of doing so

Office Manager And Consultant Considerations

Just a personal opinion but I've never been a fan of having an office manager or long term consultants in a single doctor practice. In some cases, especially multi doctor practices, either or both MAY be of help but thoroughly check their track record before hiring. Success demands much more than expensive advertising, more posters on the wall and brochures in the reception area. I feel it is normally unnecessary in a single doctor practice because a dentist should be quite capable of overseeing the business essentials and an office manager is an unneeded expense and increased overhead. In my opinion there can be only one boss and that is the dentist. If you do hire an office manager , clearly define roles and responsibilities from the outset to avoid power struggles and insure accountability. A good leader can accomplish this. As far as a consultant, listen, learn, evaluate value periodically and stand on your own as soon as possible. If a dentist lacks leadership skills necessary to guide a smooth running business and feels they need to hire someone it is imperative to make it clear from the outset who is the real boss I have seen too many cases of the office manager seemingly in control, thinking that they were the boss, and lording their position over other team members. This can produce a good deal of dissension. Remind them they are part of the team, not above the team.

In my mind, all team members carry an equal share of the work and value to practice success and should cooperate and be of equal standing. Caution office managers to make efforts to be a good team member at all times and to lead by example. The office manager should be a helping hand but they are still just an employee and final responsibility and control should be the dentists alone. I have observed cases where it seemed the dentist was so unsure of their ability and relegated too much control and became too dependent on an office manager. The question should be 'who works for who'? While some office managers are skilled in administrative tasks, they often do not possess a comprehensive knowledge of a business and the experience required to make strategic, critical decisions and often lack adequate financial oversight. They do not have an ownership mentality or financial stake and simply work for a salary. A dentist saying, "I'll just do the clinical production work and leave all the administrative issues, including hiring and firing, to the office manager" leaves them open to potential mismanagement of resources and, if given too much control, an office manager may display lack of accountability to the dentist's overall business goals.

While an office manager may increase office efficiency and relieve a great deal of burden off the dentist it is imperative they are a good fit before they are hired and are aware of their role. The dentist alone needs to be in control of financial oversight and require frequent financial reporting and evaluation of the budget. From the beginning an office manager must be given a clearly defined role and be aware of the limitations to their authority and be informed when a dentist must be consulted for certain decisions. Periodically evaluate if the money you spend on a consultant or office manager is really an effective use of money. If not then terminate their services to reduce overhead which puts more money in your pocket and learn to lead and be in control. It is not that hard!!

Daily Oversight

In any situation, the dentist must be a decisive, attentive leader and astute at keeping up with the financial aspects of the practice. It is easy to review each area's finances by informing your front office staff what you need daily, weekly or monthly. Review where you stand with weekly production and collection and expenses. Keep on top of the 30-60-90 day accounts receivables and take aggressive steps to reduce. Ask your front office for daily, weekly and monthly financial reports- production, collection, expenses and accounts receivables. There is a great deal of software available today to make your job easier in accomplishing this task.

By your practice being a well run business the end results should be financial stability, better operational efficiency, excellent patient satisfaction, excellent growth potential, high team morale, reduced staff management stress and an overall improved office culture because things are more organized and not in continual flux. If everyone knows their responsibilities and importance to the success of the practice, the schedule runs more smoothly and the dentist can realize the level of success they have always hoped for. Remember, it takes effort and leadership and organizational skills to turn a staff into a team ; big difference. Benefits include:

- Enhanced financial stability
- Improved efficiency and operational excellence
- increased patient satisfaction and loyalty
- Reduced overhead
- Stronger growth potential and practice value
- Increased team morale and staff turnover
- Clearer team responsibilities, creating a cohesive team atmosphere

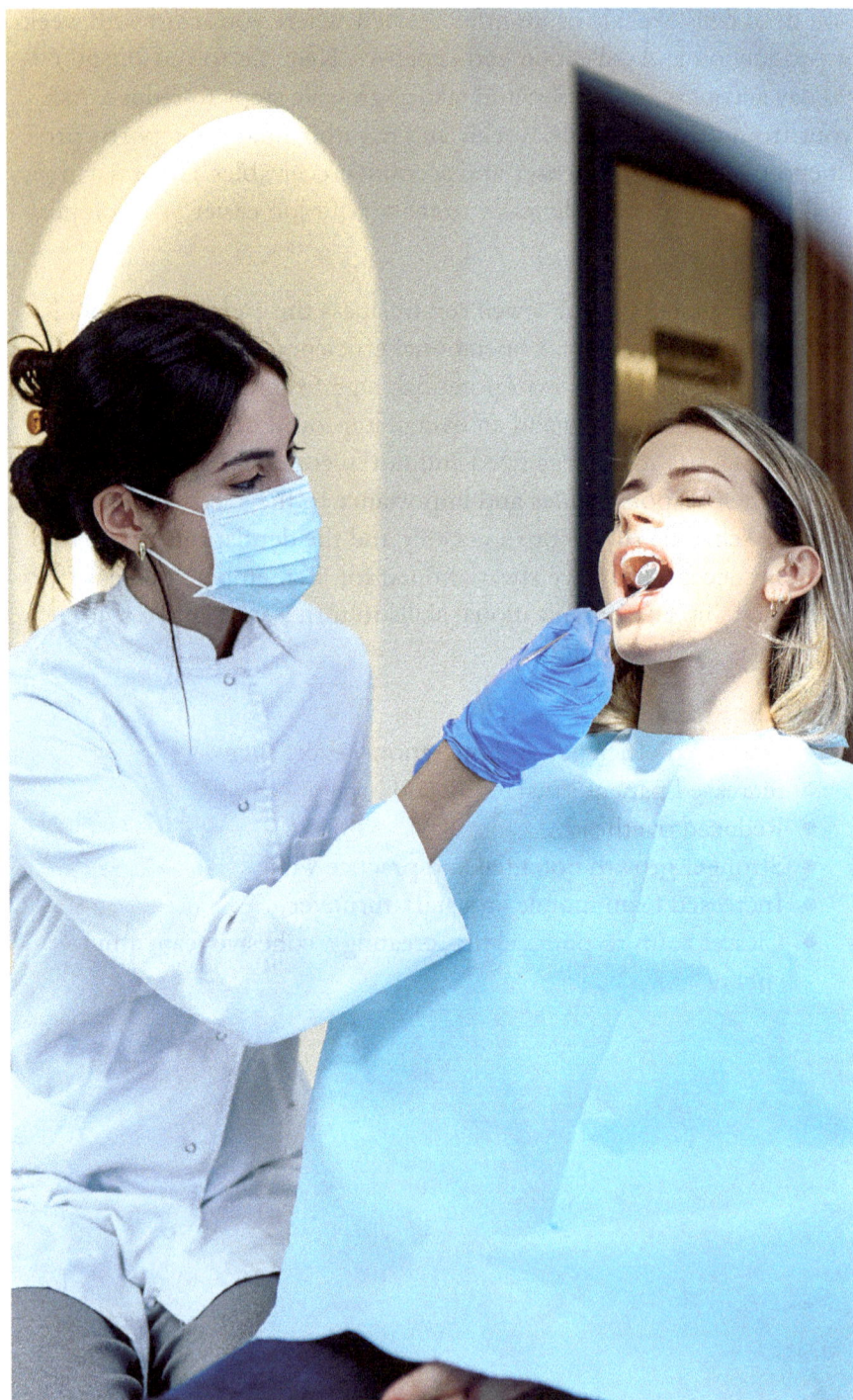

Chapter 3

General Dentistry Insights

This chapter is aimed squarely at general dentists. I occasionally serve as a volunteer clinical instructor at a major dental school and students often ask me which specialty they might pursue. My consistent reply, General Dentistry, usually confuses them as if I didn't catch the question or had left my hearing aids at home. But I mean it earnestly. I do advise them to apply for a General Practice Residency somewhere since that will put them light years ahead of the average dental school graduate when they begin to practice. Being a general dentist can be the best of all worlds. You get to perform any procedures you are comfortable with and refer the rest. Specialists are stuck with whatever walks through their door, bless them. Having a broad horizon of skills is a powerful tool that guides the path to exceptional patient care. Personally, I enjoy performing every procedure in my comfort zone. It reminds me of going to a potluck meal at church, an exciting spread of endless possibilities. As stated previously, from my early days in practice, I did everything from full mouth periodontal surgery to impacted third molars and molar endodontics. As my practice grew, I later cut back on many of those clinical offerings because my schedule was already full of restorative and other procedures but I still performed some on a case to case basis to keep me proficient. I've always offered limited ortho, fixed and removable appliances, frenectomies, tongue tie and lateral rotating flap procedures, simple extractions, tori reductions, ridge contouring, removable partials, crown and bridge, veneers, and anything I felt I could do well. If a dentist is busy and profitable doing composites, implants, crown and bridge, Invisalign, Botox or other specialty procedures they may not need to expand their repertoire, but not everyone's local demographics or economic situations allow. The idea that a dentist must have a highly specialized practice to be highly successful is inaccurate. Any dentist, whether in a bustling urban center or a small rural town, can grow a thriving, profitable practice by broadening services offered .The idea is to keep your schedule full with people who keep appointments, pay for services promptly and to refer less procedures so as to keep more income in house

Financial Chairtime Considerations

Consider for a moment what goes into a single crown procedure. There is the prepping, impressions or scanning, perhaps Cerac, temporizing, reappointing, adjusting, going through the whole procedure if it does not initially fit or sending it back to the lab for color changes plus lab fees in most cases. It can be a drawn out ordeal. Meanwhile, in the same period of time, one can complete a quadrant of composites or simple extractions, an anterior or premolar endo and a build up and have fewer potential comebacks, no lab fees, and the difference in income to chair time ratio is negligible, or sometimes even tilts in favor of the less glamorous procedures in the end. Nowadays, there is no shortage of excellent continuing education courses designed for general dentists. AGD members working towards their FAGD or MAGD certainly make a significant commitment and, as a former president of my state AGD, I'm aware of the sacrifices they make. However, a full blown pursuit of those credentials isn't for everyone. Pick an area you have interest in pursuing and go forth. The important thing is to keep your clinical skills fresh and focus on areas you feel comfortable tackling. Current endodontic techniques and chairside dental imaging, for example, make anterior and premolar root canals much simpler and highly predictable and profitable. It amazes me how some struggling practices I have worked with refer even simple extractions. They can be a substantial service and income source for the general dentist, especially if it spares patients the higher cost of sedation or specialist fees. It also tends to build loyalty, since you're saving time, money and often providing convenience and the patient can use the majority of their deductible in your office, not someone else's.

Expansion Considerations

If you're already booked solid and don't need to personally add more procedures, consider hiring an associate anyway who can expand your patient base and range of services, assuming you have the facility and staff capacity. New dentists who have completed GPR or other residencies, retired military or government personnel or experienced dentists seeking a new opportunity and proficient in expanded clinical procedures are a good pool to draw from. They can ease some stress from the owner's shoulders and increase the value of the practice and be a good possibility for purchasing the practice if the practice owner is a few short years away from retiring. They also become a built in second opinion for tough cases. Just be sure your office layout, staff levels and patient flow can support another provider without adding more chaos. Our national survey revealed that being too busy and not busy enough are both major stresses for dentists in markedly an almost equal measure. If a dentist is not busy enough and wants to increase patient load, expanding clinical offerings is one option, but remember to integrate the other strategies outlined in this book, everything from leadership to scheduling to staff harmony, because they all play a part in future success. Above all, don't settle for stagnation. If your practice situation feels unsatisfactory, take control instead of letting circumstances control you. Failure to act often leads to regrets later in life. The key is to stay proactive, adapt and keep growing, because that's what real general dentists do best!.

Reflection And Practice

- Evaluate clinical procedures currently offered and examine areas you might comfortably consider offering in the future
- Truthfully consider any hesitations and if they are realistic or should you proceed
- Calculate weekly open schedule time and lost income. Determine what procedure(s) you refer most often and concentrate on that/ those areas for possible expansion first .

Chapter 4

DENTAL PRACTICE LEADERSHIP

Several years ago I visited the practice of a close dental school classmate. He showed me around his office, introduced me to his staff and on the surface it all seemed ideal. He was an excellent clinician with an MAGD after his name. At lunch the conversation centered around his feeling that, even though on paper he had a large, successful practice, he didn't seem to be getting ahead. There was still a large home mortgage, office overhead and his schedule were out of control and staff turnover was an issue. He was always stressed and had not put away enough money to feel comfortable retiring at 65 years old as hoped and was discouraged. We had graduated 35 years earlier. Hopefully at this stage in one's career, barring health issues, contested divorce or other unforeseen, unfortunate, financially altering situations, one would be in a more stable situation personally and professionally and feel secure for the future but, unfortunately, this scenario is an all too common occurrence in our profession.

Unprepared

The majority of new dentists graduate school with minimal communication, business and leadership skills but are expected to seamlessly transition from student into being able to successfully run a practice at some point in the future. The empowerment to accomplish this goal begins with acquiring strategic management and communication skills and understanding the critical role leadership plays in building a successful dental practice. Most new graduates have never held a real job or management position, and even fewer have ever had any experience in a real world leadership role. Few can communicate effectively with others outside of their own age and socio-economic group which will not encompass the majority of their patient base and many have spent little or no time in a dental chair as a restorative patient which makes it difficult to feel empathy for the patient experience. New dentists are objectively ill-equipped for success.

Thankfully many dental schools have expanded curriculums offering more classes in practice management and the areas previously mentioned which will help new graduates be better prepared upon graduating thus providing a basic foundation upon which to build for the future.

A Business First And Foremost

As previously discussed, a dental practice is first and foremost a business. While clinical knowledge and proficiency grow exponentially with time, continuing education and hands-on experience, the other areas referenced quite often lag behind because of personal limitations and lack of real world educational opportunities. Relying on one's clinical skills alone is a sure map for eventual failure or marginal long term success. In truth, a good clinician with better than average communication, business, financial and leadership skills will consistently be more successful than a dentist depending on clinical skills alone. Becoming a good leader is the confidence builder and glue and first step necessary to accomplish competence in the other areas mentioned. A few years working as an associate can be very helpful building confidence, knowledge and clinical expertise but is often insufficient to prepare for eventual practice ownership. Younger associates should also be aware the senior dentist may not have all the answers. They should observe what the senior dentist does well, emulate and improve upon it but also note what to do, not to do or improve upon in the future as practice owners .

What Is A Leader

Having a successful, profitable and satisfying career and being able to financially and emotionally retire whenever the time feels right should be the preferred goal of every dentist. This chapter will concentrate on good leadership alone because leadership is the glue that holds a practice together.

According to Leadership expert Robin Sharma:

"Leadership is not about a title or designation. It is about impact, influence and inspiration. Impact involves getting results, influence is spreading the passion you have for your work, and a leader inspires teammates and customers alike."

John Maxwell, American author, speaker and pastor, states:

"A leader is one who knows the way, goes the way and shows the way. Leadership is not practiced so much in words as in attitude and actions. The art of communication is the language of a leader"

Alexa Chilcutt, PHD and Debbie Druey, MBA in their book *Instrumental Leadership* state:

"Research indicates the primary predictor of an organization's culture are the leadership practices of the person in charge. The leader's perspective of the organization, decision making processes and conflict management tactics have a major impact on team behavior"

I've always said that it is better to be respected than simply liked and know from experience that a good leader can achieve both. To be respected one must show respect to those they lead. If service is beneath you, leadership is beyond you! A great many of the issues that lead to burnout, (staff dysfunction, high turnover, holes in the schedule, dissatisfied, ungrateful patients etc.) along with exacerbating personal health and financial problems, may often be attributed to a lack of control. Though the uninitiated often perceive a leader as one wielding power and dominion over his/her subjects, a good leader is not hierarchical, autocratic, afraid of feedback, afraid of conflict, or above correction. Rather, a good leader leads by example and makes known that, although the final decision is theirs, the benefits to the team of which they are part is paramount. Taking control when it has not been the norm can cause negative practice disruption if the transition is about power rather than empowerment. A dentist's transformation from tepid technician to intrepid leader ought not feel like a coup, but a thoughtful and intelligent assumption of control that at once facilitates the acknowledgement of a dentist's role as team leader while enhancing each team member's sense of power and contribution. To do this, the dentist must create a vision and continually guide the team in a positive manner towards achieving a successful result. A rudderless boat uses up a lot of energy going in circles but never really goes anywhere. The idea is to have staff and patients alike buy into your vision.

Leadership Considerations

Following are some proven leadership suggestions to cultivate or enhance your ability to enjoy a smoother running office:

1. Do not delegate most or all leadership roles (contrary to what many consultants suggest) to someone else, e.g. office manager or consultant. You are the boss – act like it.

2. Be willing to seek advice and be flexible and willing to change for the better, but trust in your own common sense in decision making.

3. Exercise leadership traits through policies, consistency and example and adhere to policies you set.

4. Attitude is infectious: It starts in the AM, is contagious, but can be constructive or destructive

5. Honesty, integrity and excellent clinical skills are noticed and admired by staff and patients. Adhere to a "do unto others" attitude at all times

6. Allow your team to feel they have a vital role in practice success by considering their input and fully utilizing and acknowledging their particular skills

7. You, the doctor, are the director and producer. Your name is on the door and banknote. Never forget your role.

8. Have a "buck stops here" attitude. Let your team know you have their backs when certain situations arise. Do not shirk your duty as their leader.

9. Endeavor to stay on time. Be aware of the stress always running behind schedule has on your entire staff. This problem causes more dissent than anything else!

10. Compliment your team members when deserved. Show appreciation. Be aware of and take an interest in their life away from the office.

11. I suggest not letting your staff or patients call the doctor by their first name. You are Dr. Smith, not Kathy. Resist close social contact. It may work out sometimes but ultimately, in the long run, familiarity causes problems.

12. Be firm. I know what you are thinking, but being firm does not mean being dictatorial. This does not diminish your kindness or caring attitude towards staff or patients but they must know you mean what you say! Remember, it is better to be respected than simply liked. A good leader accomplishes both.

13. Be the first to arrive and last to leave when possible. During short daylight times never leave the office until all your team members are safely on their way. It is your duty!!!!!

14. Lead by example. If running behind or just a very busy day, empty a trash can, pick up debris, help clean an operatory. They know you do not have to do this but never ask an employee to do something you are unwilling to do. You are head of the team but also a part of the team. You will be surprised how this positively helps morale

Pace Yourself

For many these suggestions may seem daunting, even harsh, and many dentists have already dug a hole they may have difficulty digging out of. Transition may not be easy and certainly not instantaneous but remember, if one continues doing the same old thing, one continues getting the same old results as Einstein stated. Pick one or two suggestions and then ease into more as you feel comfortable and can see positive results. Take control and be a leader. What do you have to lose!!

Therefore ask yourself; do you run your practice or does your practice run you? In our National Survey on Dental Practice Stress, some of the stressors like running behind schedule and constraint time pressures or being too busy or not busy enough we expected but staff issues and dissatisfied , ungrateful patients made the top ten as well. We realized that these and many other significant stressors from the survey could be traced to a lack of leadership skills and not being able to control circumstances on the part of the practitioner. This does not infer the dentist is not a highly qualified clinician, a nice person, respected and even almost venerated in the community. It simply means that dentists are somehow expected to acquire necessary skills through osmosis. There is a huge difference between being a boss and a leader. Therefore it is time to overcome fears and take charge of one's own destiny . Making positive changes and enforcing them effectively has a profound positive effect on your team and the quality of your future practice experiences.

Benefits Of Good Leadership

The following benefits of good leadership are not exclusive or exhaustive but do highlight many of the benefits.

1. More self confidence and reduced need for others in decision making

2. A willingness to face problems rather than run away from them

3. Reduced stress because you now control circumstances rather than allowing circumstances to control you

4. Improved outlook for the future

5. Reduced fear of change and making changes in your personal and professional life

6. A leader becomes part of the solution rather than part of the problem

7. Staff display more confidence in and respect for you

8. Improved confidence improves communication skills with team and patients

9. Increased productivity

10. Inspires team initiative. A good leader trains personnel well and gives them leeway to make decisions within reason which greatly improves morale and builds confidence and pride in team members

11. Reduces staff turnover

12. Good leadership is contagious and bonds the entire team together. They encourage one another and are proud of their role and contributions to the practice success.

In conclusion, effective leadership demands compassion, humility and a genuine commitment to the team's best interests. Your team's loyalty and dedication will know no bounds. Obviously one does not morph from a Don Knots "Barney Fyfe" into a Dwayne " The Rock" Johnson overnight but we all must start somewhere. There are a lot of in between levels that may be considered successful so take one step at a time, do not become discouraged, persist and set sights on a better future. Commit to becoming a leader, embrace change and shape your practice into one that provides lasting professional satisfaction, financial security and personal fulfillment.

Reflection And Practice

- After reading this chapter evaluate your personal circumstances
- Consider one or two areas you might concentrate on and make changes. Be consistent. Over a month's period if you note positive changes add one or more ideas to work on.
- If your efforts are not appreciated or accepted by a team member/members, then it might be time to make some employee changes. Do not go backwards and accept defeat. Put the blame where it belongs.

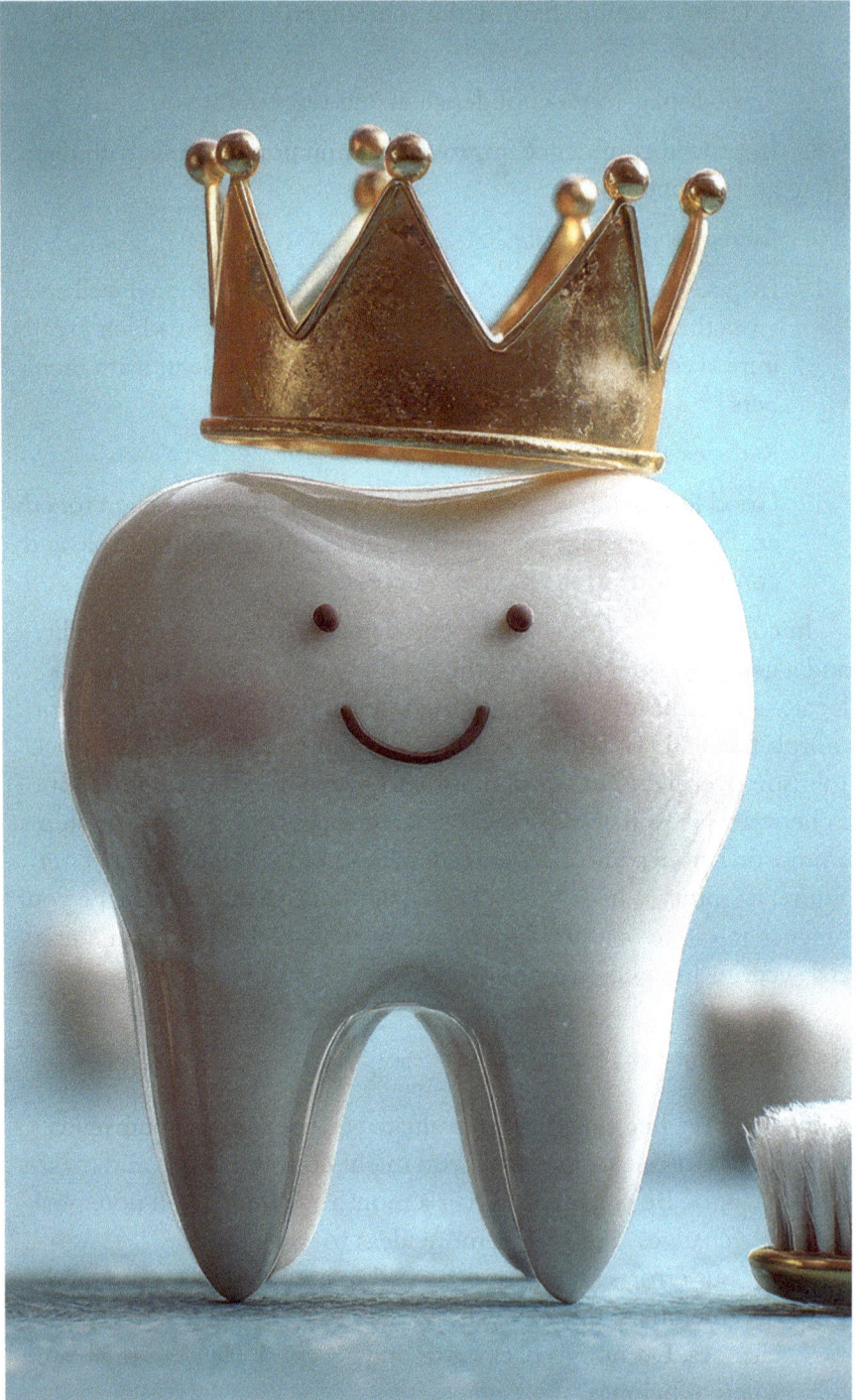

Chapter 5

PRACTICE PERCEPTION
TIMEX OR ROLEX

Perception Is Reality

For most people, perception is reality. Success is not just about dentistry-it's about the experience. If patients think you are the best dentist in the world, then—until proven otherwise—you are. Many highly skilled clinicians with impressive credentials often wonder why they are underbooked, their practice seems stagnant, and they are not where they wanted to be in life while another dentist down the street, with minimal required continuing education and no special designations, is constantly busy, hires an associate, and even limits new-patient intake. The answer typically comes down to perception and highly effective internal marketing. It's less about clinical expertise and more about personality, communication skills, overall practice environment, and consistent, exceptional experiences from the moment patients first encounter your practice to the moment they leave. In other words, a well-run business where the entire team understands that the real secret to success is selling oneself before trying to sell one's product which, in our case, are our dental services.

Why Touch Points Matter

We call this principle Touch Point Choreography. Every point of contact—from the website to the front desk greeting, from the operatory experience to the checkout—must be positive and memorable. There can be no weak links in the process. Of course, excellent clinical care must back up that warm experience, but let's be honest, patients expect quality care to be the baseline—what truly distinguishes one practice from another is how consistently you exceed their expectations at every step. I challenge you to read your or other dentists' reviews and find "Dr. Smith is wonderful! The margins of her crowns are so precise that, with good oral hygiene, chances of future decay around the crown are minimal" or "Dr. Jones took such care when he filled some deep cavities and placed insulation on the prep floor to help reduce sensitivity." Rather, you will see comments talking about how friendly your staff is, how everyone made them feel like family, or how the dentist explains things well. Sadly, most patients think a dentist does a great job if everything feels smooth to the tongue, looks good, and the dentist inflicts little or no pain. You get my drift.

Timex Versus Rolex

Both Timex and Rolex are reliable timepieces. Both watches keep good time. Timex even offers some attractive, pricier models, but only one becomes an heirloom to be locked in a safe when not in use and considered a tragedy if lost or stolen. In the end, a Timex is just a watch and if lost or stolen can be easily replaced. Transcend mere function and you become the treasure your patient holds forever special.

Ask yourself: Do patients treat your practice like a Timex—replaceable and ordinary? Or do they see it as a Rolex—exceptional, valued, and irreplaceable? Rolex practices inspire patient loyalty, generate on-time payments, earn heartfelt referrals, and foster a sense of genuine emotional loss if the dentist retires or no longer practices for any reason. When you're perceived as a Rolex practice, you hardly worry about the state of the economy or the competition down the street. People are proud to be your patient, never want to go elsewhere, can't wait to tell others, and never want you to retire. Achieving Rolex status requires vision and is only accomplished through the good leadership efforts of the dentist.

Building a Rolex Practice

1. Focus on Internal Marketing

A Rolex-level reputation doesn't come from flashy ads or designer uniforms alone—it's driven by internal marketing. That means delivering the "wow factor" at every step. If a new patient's first visit is less than ideal, they may tell many others about their negative experience. On the flip side, if they're blown away, they become an instant ambassador for your practice.

2. Perfect the First Impression

Online Presence: Your website should be attractive, informative, and easy to navigate, conveying friendliness, care, and professionalism.

Initial Phone Call: People should sense a smiling, eager-to-help staff member on the other end, not an impersonal automated menu. Nothing beats a friendly voice saying "Good morning. Dr. Jones' office. This is Donna. How can I help you?"

Office Exterior & Reception: Make sure the property is clean, welcoming, and aesthetically pleasing. Regularly walk in through the main entrance to see what patients see and even smell. Inside, create a warm, comfortable reception area (not a "waiting room") with inviting lighting, nice furniture, plants, lovely pictures, up-to-date reading materials, and even an area for coffee, tea, and bottled water. A children's play area is a real bonus if space permits.

3. Choreograph the Patient Experience

A positive patient journey doesn't happen by chance—it's the result of intentional planning and attention to detail. From the initial greeting to the final goodbye, each step should reinforce your commitment to comfort, respect, and genuine concern.

Making Patients Feel Special

Warm Welcome: Address each patient by title (Mr., Ms., Mrs., Dr.)

at all times. We even refer to children as "Mr. Bobby" or "Miss Katie." This simple gesture conveys respect and sets the tone for a professional relationship. I personally dislike some young person opening the door and calling "Gary" and then pointing to a room down the hall.

Personal Escort: Rather than calling names from across the reception area or pointing down a hallway, the team member initially seating the patient should call the patient's name, make eye contact, introduce themself with a smile and warm personal greeting, and personally guide them to the operatory. Every patient should feel like a VIP who deserves your full attention. I always told my staff I wanted people to feel someone was throwing rose petals in their path and trumpets were heralding their presence every step of their visit.

Set an Enthusiastic Tone: A friendly smile and a genuine "We're glad you're here" can make them feel appreciated before they ever sit in the chair.

Operatory Prep

Clear Expectations: Once the patient is seated, explain the planned procedures for the appointment and ask if they have any questions. Knowing the plan eases anxiety.

Physical Comfort: Attend to the patient's comfort. Ideally adjust their headrest, offer a blanket if chilly, give them the TV remote or offer a magazine if they will be waiting for a short time, and inform them noise-canceling headphones are available if they wish. Even if a patient declines, simply offering underscores your concern for their comfort. If the patient is to be left alone for any period of time, never leave them lying back with the light in their eyes—an all too common experience in offices I have worked with.

Emotional Reassurance: A calm, empathetic demeanor works wonders for nervous patients. Ask if they have any concerns and listen attentively. Small gestures—like a gentle touch on the shoulder—can help patients feel supported and safe.

Doctor Presentation

Professional Appearance and Demeanor: Your attire, body language, and tone of voice are all part of your "presentation." Patients care less about the clinical details of your training and more about how at ease you make them feel. As Will Rogers stated: "You never get a second chance to make a first impression." Every day of my practice life I have worn a dress shirt, tie, and white clinic jacket. There is never any doubt who has just entered the room. Remember, at every step in the appointment, exceed expectations. How a doctor looks and presents themself has little to do with clinical proficiency, but it does make a positive impact on the patient initially.

Confidence Without Arrogance: Be self-assured in your clinical expertise but remain approachable. Eye contact, a handshake or warm greeting, and an empathetic smile go a long way in building trust.

In our chapter entitled "Successful, Non-Stressful Treatment Plan Presentation and Acceptance," we discuss how to structure the initial exam to give the patient a sense of exceptional value, to build trust, and to never have the patient feel pressured about treatment. We instill feelings of confidence in our ability to care for their future dental needs.

Listen More, Talk Less

Open-Ended Questions: Encourage patients to describe their concerns, previous experiences, and goals for their dental health. Their answers can reveal underlying anxieties or priorities that might not surface otherwise.

Validation and Empathy: Acknowledge their feelings ("I understand how this could be stressful…") before responding. This helps patients feel heard and valued.

Collaborative Treatment Planning: By actively listening, you can propose treatment options that align with both clinical needs and the patient's personal comfort level, resulting in higher acceptance and long-term loyalty. Many patients do not return for treatment because they have had a deer-in-the-headlights shock when presented their treatment plan. In extreme need cases, present treatment in stages, attempting to get the patient's basic dental foundation in order before moving on to the next sequence. This offers additional time to build a personal relationship of trust and confidence in your abilities before proceeding to the next, more comprehensive and expensive phase of treatment and increases treatment plan acceptance.

A Memorable Exit

Positive Send-Off: The impression you make as patients leave is just as important as how you greet them. Genuinely thank them for trusting you with their care.

Mind the Audience: Patients leaving most often pass by those in the reception area. A happy patient, smiling and chatting with the team, can have a reassuring effect on those waiting their turn.

Smooth Checkout: Make scheduling follow-up appointments and processing payments a breeze. A confusing or drawn-out checkout process can leave a sour final impression.

Encourage Feedback and Referrals: Let them know you value their opinion and would appreciate any referrals. This not only boosts loyalty but also signals that you're confident in the experience you provided.

Why It Matters

When patients feel welcomed, heard, and genuinely cared for at every step, they're far more likely to trust your recommendations, accept treatment, and refer others. By choreographing each phase of the visit—from warm greetings to thoughtful goodbyes—you transform ordinary office visits into memorable, positive experiences that set your practice apart. That is why it is so important to hire only team members who have the personality and natural care and concern for others so they can align with your philosophy of patient care.

Ultimately, you're not just treating teeth—you're caring for people. The better they feel about their time with you, the more likely they are to become loyal patients who happily share their experiences with family and friends.

In Review: Always Exceed Expectations

Each touch point should build trust. Eliminate any sense of pressure, explain options clearly, and show genuine concern for patient comfort, finances, and well-being. When people leave your office, they should feel they've had the best dental (or any business) experience of their lives—and be excited to tell friends and family about it. They should get a sense that their coming to your office was the highlight of your day.

Maintain Ongoing Care & Follow-up

A simple but impactful step is calling patients who present for the first time for emergency treatment or potentially experience pain after any treatment. I have done this every night of my practice life. A simple "Ms. Davis, this is Dr. Stough. I just wanted to see how you are doing and if you have any questions following today's treatment." It only takes a few minutes, can be done on your cell phone while driving home, and leaves a lasting impression of genuine care—further cementing your status as a Rolex-level practice. It also lessens the possibility of your returning to the office at night for a patient bleeding or in pain since you can reiterate post-op instructions. I always have staff follow up with a call the next day. It is amazing the referrals this generates.

Lead Your Team to Rolex Status

Regardless of where you are in your career, you can elevate your practice's perception. It requires leadership and a team fully committed to exceeding patient expectations at each phase of the visit. Emphasize these focal points:

- Website excellence
- Friendly, personal phone reception
- A clean, inviting exterior and warm reception area
- Respectful greetings and professional escort to the operatory
- Comfortable and efficient operatory experience by a mindful, caring team
- A doctor who inspires confidence through both appearance and behavior
- A non-stressful treatment plan discussion
- A smooth checkout process with genuine appreciation for the patient

When you get every member of your staff aligned on these goals, you'll cultivate an atmosphere that not only meets but exceeds patient expectations—every single time.

Timex or Rolex? The choice is yours, and with the right strategy and leadership, you can shine as a Rolex practice that never worries about losing patients or weathering economic storms. Exceed expectations at every turn, and watch your schedule stay full, your revenue grow, and your patients become devoted advocates for your practice.

Reflection And Practice

- Walk into your office tomorrow as if you were a new patient. What do you notice? What do you see, hear , feel and even smell?
- Choose one small touch point- like phone greetings or followup calls- and improve it this month.
- Ask your team: " What one thing can we do to make patients feel more valued.

Chapter 6

Minimize Mistakes And Reduce The Stress Of Hiring Staff

Hiring staff for your dental practice is like casting actors for an ensemble play—every member has both starring and supporting roles at various points during a patient's visit. Two key principles must guide your choices: consistency and congruence. Although this sounds simple enough, staff-related issues consistently rank among the top stressors dentists face. Ideally, if a team is dysfunctional, you might fantasize about clearing the slate and starting fresh. Realistically, that's not practical. The best solution is to refine your hiring process to avoid repeating past mistakes. Hiring is not simply filling a vacancy; it's shaping your practice's future. Careful assembly of a team creates a less stressed office atmosphere and is a great benefit to practice success. Here are strategies to help you succeed:

Clearly Define the Role

When seeking new staff, clearly outline the position—whether full or part-time, required experience, computer skills, language requirements, and interpersonal skills. Describe your ideal candidate with terms like dependable, outgoing, caring, and service-oriented.

Effective Screening Methods

Instead of initially receiving countless resumes, designate a team member to pre-screen applicants over the phone. A screener can quickly evaluate basic qualifications, communication skills, phone etiquette, and ask questions as needed. If an applicant inquires about salary and/or benefits, the screener should respond that those subjects are based on previous experience, job suitability, and interview results. Invite promising applicants to pick up an application in person, allowing a visual and interpersonal evaluation before granting an interview. Although an extra step, this significantly reduces wasted time. Simply having resumes sent online or to the office or PO Box address is fraught with problems because too many unqualified people require wasted time and effort culling from real possibilities. Always thoroughly and personally check references, especially former employers, before proceeding further.

Where to Look

Explore multiple avenues to find great candidates, including online recruitment services, current and former staff recommendations, local hygiene and auxiliary schools, dental supply representatives, recruitment firms, and even traditional newspaper ads.

Experienced vs. Trainable

Hiring experienced staff might seem ideal as they require less immediate training, but beware—experienced candidates may resist change (old dogs, new tricks scenario), may compare unfavorably with past positions, or struggle with your office's pace and procedures. All experiences are not the same. You do not want to hire an assistant who cannot stand the sight of blood if you perform surgical procedures which their previous dentist did not, or a front office individual who will be tasked with discussing financial issues or pursuing accounts receivable who psychologically cannot handle the task. Consider instead hiring trainable, motivated individuals who possess excellent interpersonal skills and enthusiasm for learning. Many of my best hires—such as Patti, who managed a local Tastee Freeze, and Deanna from customer service—had no dental background but excelled due to their attitudes and adaptability. This works best when a new hire considers the job a step up.

Cross-Training and Back-Up Plans

Unfortunately, many new hires are the result of a knee-jerk reaction when suddenly a practice is left without the services of an employee for any reason. This often leads to rushed hires and subsequent disasters. To prevent this, cross-train your existing team as much as possible so they can fill in when needed. Additionally, maintain a pool of reliable temporary support—such as retired hygienists or trained external assistants—ready to step in on short notice. We trained a young lady who did not want a permanent position in assisting and front desk procedures. She was available on short notice and as a fill-in for staff on vacation. This keeps your practice running smoothly, even in unexpected circumstances.

Careful Background Checks and Red Flags

Again, be certain as you narrow down your list of possibilities to always follow up on resumes. Do not simply accept what is written. Call former employers and, if you sense they are hesitant or holding back opinions, simply ask if the position opened in their office and the candidate in question was available, would they hire them—a simple yes or no. You might be surprised by their answer. Pay attention to red flags like frequent job changes or unexplained employment gaps. Checking social media profiles can also reveal valuable insights into the candidate's judgment and personal life habits. Remember, these people represent your office even when they are not at work.

Interviewing

Prepare specific interview questions in advance. Look carefully at employment histories, asking candidates directly about job transitions, their strengths and weaknesses, and scenarios they find challenging. If a dentist is uncomfortable with the interview process, they might consider having another trusted staff member join them during the interview for an additional perspective. I suggest never letting an office manager or other employee make a final hiring decision. That is the doctor's responsibility. When you have narrowed down possibilities, having your team take promising candidate(s) out to lunch to assess compatibility has prevented costly mistakes in my practice. They are the ones who will work with the new employee, and their input can be very beneficial. Some sample interview questions might include:

1. Reason for seeking an employment change (immediately dismiss anyone who trashes a former employer).

2. Tell me about your previous work experience and duties.

3. Tell me a little about yourself and your background (interesting negative responses at times).

4. What traits can you bring to this office to enhance efficiency and continued success?

5. What are your weaknesses? What are your strengths?

6. How would former co-workers describe you?

7. Describe your ability to relate to others.

8. What traits do you find unsettling when dealing with co-workers and the public in general?

9. Would you be willing to cross-train in other areas? What are your long-term goals?

10. What are you seeking insofar as hourly compensation and benefits? (May price themselves out of contention.)

11. Would you be willing to agree to a 60-day employment trial period? (If required.)

12. What questions can I answer?

These are simply suggestions, and the reader should make their own list. Having a list of questions and "not shooting from the hip" helps the doctor to cover all pertinent areas in an orderly manner.

Making the Offer

Once you've selected your preferred candidate, provide a formal written offer outlining their responsibilities, salary, benefits, schedule, and expectations—including cross-training and an initial evaluation period if agreed upon. Clear documentation prevents misunderstandings and provides legal protection should issues arise later. Have them sign a document that they have read and agree with your office policy and job description manuals.

Handling Issues with Staff

Even with careful hiring, staff issues can and will occur, often stemming from their personal lives. One of my most dependable assistants began having performance issues after marital problems led her to substance abuse. Despite counseling and offering support, the situation didn't improve, and I had to let her go. Situations like these illustrate why clearly documented disciplinary procedures are essential (see the chapter "Reducing Staff Stress" for more guidance).

While no system is foolproof, following these guidelines will greatly reduce the stress related to hiring and staffing, making your dental practice more efficient, pleasant, and successful. Once you hire , lead with clarity. Set expectations, reward excellence and confront problems early.

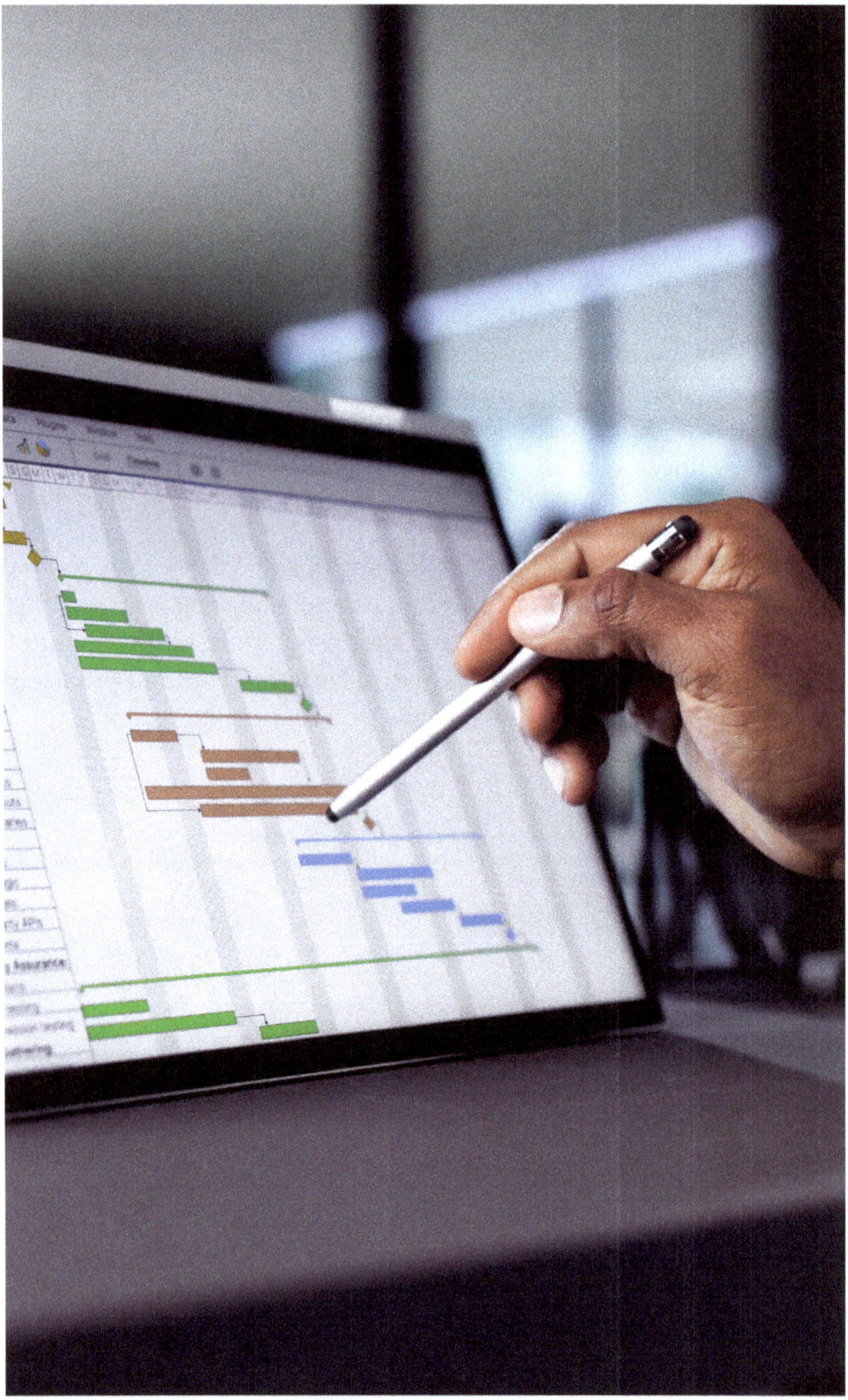

Chapter 7

CONTROLLING THE OFFICE SCHEDULE

In our two national surveys on dental practice stress, the number one stressor was "running behind schedule," followed closely by "constant time pressures." Ranked fourth was "dissatisfied, ungrateful patients". These three issues, along with several others, can significantly be reduced if the dentist and staff proactively control the schedule rather than allowing the schedule and patient demands control them. A wise dentist schedules for peace, not panic. Learn to control your appointment book before your next meltdown, or it will happily control you!

Admittedly, no one can completely eliminate running behind schedule or dissatisfied patients. Dentistry involves imperfect humans working on imperfect humans, using imperfect materials under often unpredictable conditions. A cusp fracturing unexpectedly or an inadvertent pulp exposure can disrupt anyone's schedule. Still, our primary objective must always be to minimize these situations through proactive scheduling and planning.

A Brief Illustration

Early in my practice there was Mrs. Goss (not her real name), the patient straight from Hades. She entered my practice before I knew enough to close the proverbial barn door. Initially, like many young dentists starting a practice, anyone with a pulse seemed like a suitable patient. Bills needed to be paid, little discretion was initially applied, and as new meat for the slaughter, my share of undesirables slipped through. Obviously, problem patients are not just the bane of new practices. Many long-established practices have tolerated the problem much too long as well but lack the courage to face the issue head-on. The old adages "No guts, no glory" as well as FDR's "The only thing we have to fear is fear itself" stick out here! The number four stressor on our survey was "Dissatisfied, ungrateful patients." You can be assured that problem patients represent a high percentage of these cases. Mrs. Goss soon became a major stressor each time we saw her name on the schedule. She complained about trivial things—our music choices, the taste of the water, or if we were five minutes late seating her or 5 minutes early if she was reading a book or watching a favorite TV program. Her husband, bless him, was kind and patient, the exact opposite of her personality. We did everything we could, but the problem was Mrs. Goss alone.

I worried about dismissing Mrs. Goss, given her connections at a large local employer from which we'd received many patients. There was the concern she would badmouth the practice, but after much deliberation, courage prevailed and I sent her a dismissal letter. She responded emotionally, shocked by our decision. I explained the facts and realized I had made a wise decision when many patients from her workplace later confided in us that they couldn't believe we'd tolerated her as long as we had! As far as dismissals, you can be assured others know what these people are like and will take that into consideration should they try to besmirch your name. Mr. Goss, the dear man, remained a loyal patient, and our practice atmosphere dramatically improved.

The lesson here is clear: you, as the dentist, must control your schedule, set firm rules from the start, and dismiss patients who habitually fail appointments, arrive late, disrespect staff, or refuse to pay. Let them go make another dentist's life miserable. You'll discover that dismissing difficult patients will likely enhance your practice reputation rather than harm it. It matters little how many patients you have or how far your practice is scheduled out if 25% of the patients do not show up for appointments, are unwilling to follow rules or pay on time, and make your life miserable.

Scheduling Strategies for Success:

A significant scheduling problem occurs because appointment schedulers typically don't understand clinical procedures unless they previously served as assistants. Thus, educating schedulers and periodically cross-training them is essential. Train your scheduler thoroughly on the duration and complexity of various procedures and how to distinguish between real and perceived emergencies and how to handle each scenario properly. They must also understand how hygiene visits impact your schedule, particularly if you need to examine the patient, and the difficulty of the doctor's current case if sedation or other factors require their uninterrupted attention.

Avoid overpacking your schedule, as this only increases stress and dissatisfaction among patients and staff, often negatively impacting practice revenue. It may seem counterintuitive, but sometimes less is more—more effective, more profitable, and far less stressful. Must-see walk-ins must be informed they may receive palliative treatment only in most cases. Late patients must be rescheduled in many cases as necessary.

Often the issue of a packed schedule is that the practice is too busy and the scheduler does not know where to put people, so they stick them in anywhere. I have consulted in practices where a one-hour composite appointment had a shorter procedure on the side plus the doctor was expected to check two hygienists. This is not the way to practice. It affects quality, increases the possibility of dissatisfied patients, and minimizes relationship building. It also stresses the heck out of the entire team on a daily basis! The false concept that packing more people into the schedule makes more money is a joke. If too busy, hire an associate or cease accepting new patients for a short period. I had to do it twice in my first 5 years in practice, and while it may have been a benefit to other dentists in the area in the short term, it never hurt our bottom line, and the floodgates opened once we resumed accepting new patients again.

Constantly running over into the lunch hour or at quitting time places a great deal of stress on the entire team if it is a common occurrence. The dentist and staff NEED a full lunch break to take a breath and attempt to recharge a bit. After a long day, people are ready to go home and leave the day's often torrid pace behind and resume a normal life. Do not be afraid to schedule a 15-minute buffer period before lunch and at the end of the day because most often your schedule will be running behind that amount or more, and you need the time to catch up. Mondays often have their greater share of emergencies { or perceived emergencies} because many caring patients do not want to bother the doctor over the weekend but on Monday morning they want something done!! Therefore we have always blocked out 45 minutes in the morning and afternoon.Without fail the time is always utilized. You will not lose money, and everyone, including the dentist, will be much happier.

Morning Meetings Are Essential

Morning meetings are crucial. They should NEVER be skipped. Have a fixed agenda and designated facilitator so things do not go off track and waste valuable time. A well-run meeting should never take more than 15-20 minutes. Briefly reviewing your upcoming week's schedule beforehand the week prior or on Monday morning allows you to identify and address potential scheduling conflicts/challenges in advance. Review the day's schedule, follow-up treatment inquiries, problem patients and patient special needs, and areas of possible conflict/bottleneck during the day. A well-run morning meeting improves communication between all areas, giving a big picture of the day's events and improving coordination and cooperation and keeping the schedule running more smoothly. If time allows, supply or equipment concerns may be addressed, noted, and attended to at a later time so as not to lose control of the meeting timewise.

The Importance of a Call List:

A well-managed call list is essential. Use it effectively to fill schedule gaps and cancellations. I never schedule lab cases in advance. They are a great and usually appreciated way to fill gaps quickly since patients are happy to go to the next step as soon as possible. Patients often appreciate being called earlier than their appointed times if you are scheduled out a long way. Categorize your call list clearly by procedure, appointment length, patient preference for days, times, rainy days, and required notice. Holes in the schedule are financially devastating on a yearly basis if the issue is not planned for and addressed proactively to minimize them.

Appointment Confirmations:

Patients are informed in the beginning that two no-shows or repeated late shows may be reason for dismissal from the practice. Obviously considerations are made on a case by case basis. They are informed that, as a courtesy, we will make every effort to remind them electronically and by phone, but in the end, the responsibility is theirs alone. Make sure to confirm appointments electronically several days in advance as well as by phone as the time nears, and follow up with a personal call for cancellations or if no response is received. There are platforms available that can issue appointment reminders and confirm appointments and even allow the patient to reschedule. Always follow up on cancellations, the reason for canceling, and do not let patients fall through the cracks. Another effective strategy is to assign a staff member (compensated appropriately) to handle confirmations remotely in the evening. If someone cancels, they can immediately go to the call list and fill that time. This ensures fewer surprises, dramatically reduces last-minute cancellations, and is a huge financial benefit.

Consider the financial impact of just one unfilled appointment slot per day, four days a week—calculate what this lost production equates to over a full year.

Points to Ponder in Scheduling Control:

1. Clearly communicate rules and expectations to the patient in their welcome letter and instructions to the scheduler from the outset.
2. Dismiss problematic patients decisively.

3. Educate your scheduler thoroughly about procedures, emergencies, and optimal scheduling practices.

4. Understand that overbooking does not always equal increased income and increases stress.

5. Always maintain control over the schedule—offer specific appointment times rather than allowing patients to dictate as much as possible.

6. Make morning meetings a top priority.

7. Implement 15-minute flex periods each day.

8. Use a well-structured call list consistently.

9. Confirm appointments and promptly fill openings and reschedule patients.

10. Consider evening confirmation calls to maintain a robust schedule.

By adopting these strategies, you will reduce stress, increase productivity, enhance patient satisfaction, and improve your practice's financial health.

Reflection And Practice

- Have the scheduler keep notes by category on issues that arise. Review after 30 days and concentrate on making improvements in those areas.
- As soon as the schedule allows, begin blocking off 15 minutes before lunch and quitting time and 45 minutes Monday AM and PM for a 30 day period and measure it's effectiveness in reducing stress and running over schedule.

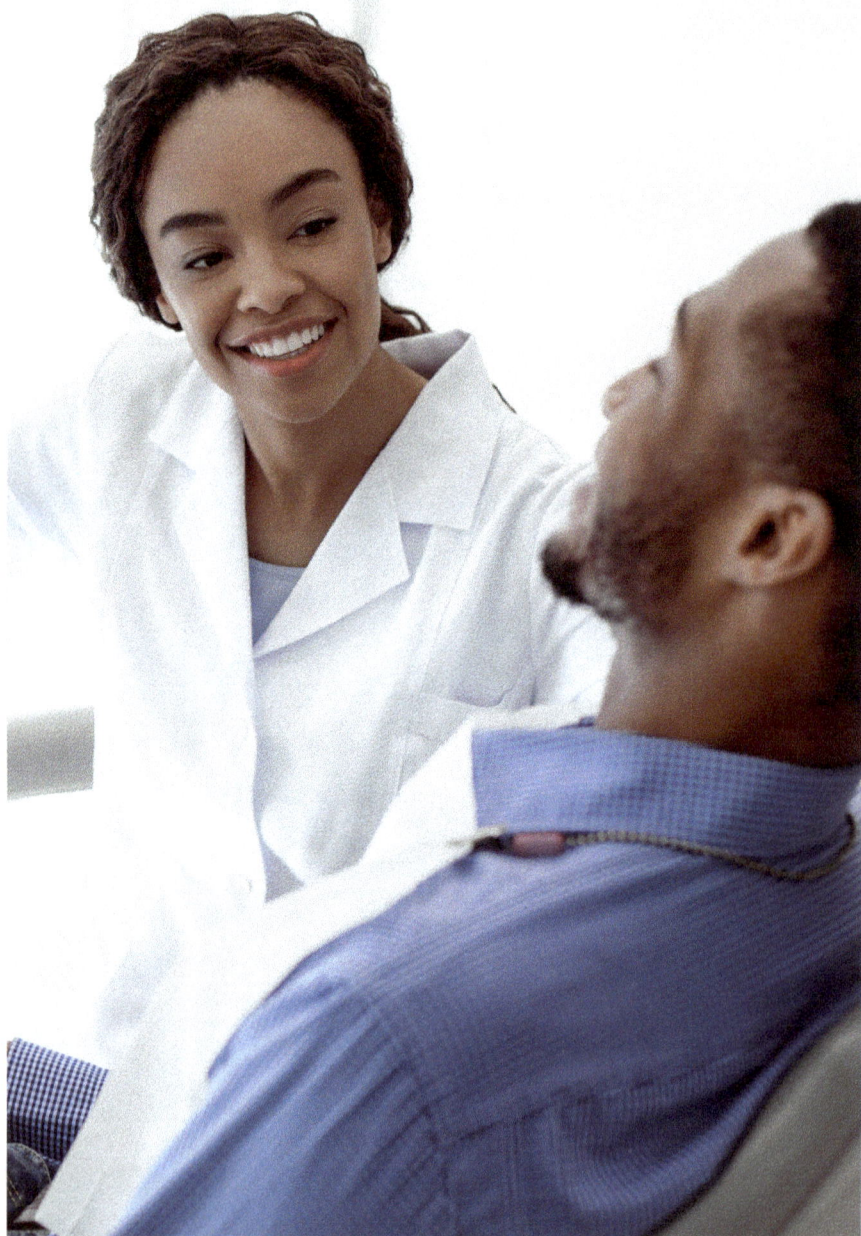

Chapter 8

Effective Internal Marketing Methods

Teddy Roosevelt stated "People don't care how much you know until they know how much you care". No advertising delivers more potent results than when patients readily refer family, friends and acquaintances to your practice.These people arrive at your office with a positive sense of trust from the very beginning. Every dentist should make up their mind what kind of patient they want in their practice. It is a fact that good patients tend to refer potentially good patients. The quantity of patients in a practice is not as important as the quality. It is better to be scheduled a month in advance with great patients who show , pay on time and are pleasant during their visit than to be scheduled further out with people who do not meet these criteria. Some sources state that 60 or 70% of new patients to a practice are from referrals. It can be higher. Some offices heavily solicit patients to refer others. That kind of more aggressive approach never suited me, but if it works for you, continue.. My approach has always been a highly successful soft sell ; simply exceeding expectations at all times and the rest works itself out. With each patient referral we send a nice thank you card telling them how honored we are by their faith and trust and willingness to refer others and include a Starbucks gift card.. Patients are appreciative!

One Patient At A Time

My thoughts have always been one patient at a time. I am naturally a people person and have always had a service attitude towards others.I probably would have been a great Butler and learned early on that one's attitude, if genuine, can also be financially beneficial. While working at a grocery store during high school, we would bag groceries and help carry them out for people.The more cheerful my demeanor, saying yes, ma'am and no, ma'am, and being courteous meant bigger tips. Often I had customers ask for me before they checked out. As a waiter in college, I found giving excellent service with a friendly, cheerful attitude had the same end result.

My goal from the first day in practice was to please every patient so well that they would tell five others. Starting with two operatories, one assistant and my wife at the front desk in an 800 square foot office, within 3 months I had hired a hygienist. Three years later I quit seeing new patients for several months and began construction on a new five operatory office, hired a second hygienist and eventually an associate. This was not a result of a lack of other dentists in our area but simply internal marketing and patient referrals. It was unavoidable that in the beginning I pleased some not so stellar patients, but over time we either educated them to become good patients or dismissed them. As I state in another chapter, never hesitate to dismiss someone fearing they will give your office negative reviews. Your good reputation overshadows a periodic poor review and others are well aware of what the person who gave you the review is like..

Never be hesitant to ask patients for referrals but do not hit them over the head with a request. Rather, when a patient has a great experience with me or a hygienist, I will say with a big smile " I am so glad you are happy with today's visit. Just remember, if you have a good experience in our office please always feel free to tell others. If not please tell me before you tell others"

Dentists attract patients in different ways. If large billboards, patient referral rewards or other marketing tools have been effective, then by all means continue. The only problem with this approach is you often do not know what kind of person will walk through the door while internal marketing and good patient referrals results in better quality patients. If you feel the need to hire a consultant then by all means do so but perform an evaluation of their effectiveness every several months to see if the investment is really paying off. Often it does not. Otherwise, dismiss them, save the money and concentrate on what we discuss in this chapter.

Involved Team Members

Be sure to instruct your team to encourage referrals as well. The dentist is not always present to hear positive comments from patients. When a patient shares their pleasure over a current or previous experience, have your team members reply " I am so happy to hear you say that. You know, Dr.Stough always loves when good patients like you refer others because good patients refer good patients. Feel free to share your satisfaction with others. That means a lot to him" One might think satisfied patients would always do so on their own accord but a friendly reminder always helps. Leveraging existing patients to attract new ones through word of mouth referrals and testimonies is cost effective and personal. Encouraging online testimonials is also a must since the first contact some patients make with your office is online. Every Christmas and every anniversary of our practice opening we placed a photo of our entire team online and in the local paper thanking patients for their trust and loyalty and always received a great deal of positive feedback as well as a number of new patients.

Going Beyond

We discuss this further in another chapter but every evening of my practice life I have called patients.. Not every patient of course but any patient who may have undergone a procedure that had a potential for post op pain as well as emergency patients and inquired about their status. It is a great opportunity to review instructions, thus lessening the necessity of a late night office return , and seldom takes more than 15 minutes. It is so easy nowadays . Simply have your receptionist give you a readout of these patients names and phone numbers and most can be contacted on your way driving home, Have your staff follow up with a call the next day. This habit alone has been a great source of referrals over the years.

Ensuring each patient has an experience that " exceeds expectations" during their first visit to your office and continuing that trend at each following visit in the future is undeniably the most effective method of internal marketing and patient referrals.

Having a practice with a quality patient base is so important because it is less stressful in so many ways for you and your team. Good internal marketing is a cost effective means to build trust, strengthen relationships, improve case acceptance and create a self -sustaining referral engine. Therefore, stress internal marketing at every opportunity and enjoy the results of your efforts.

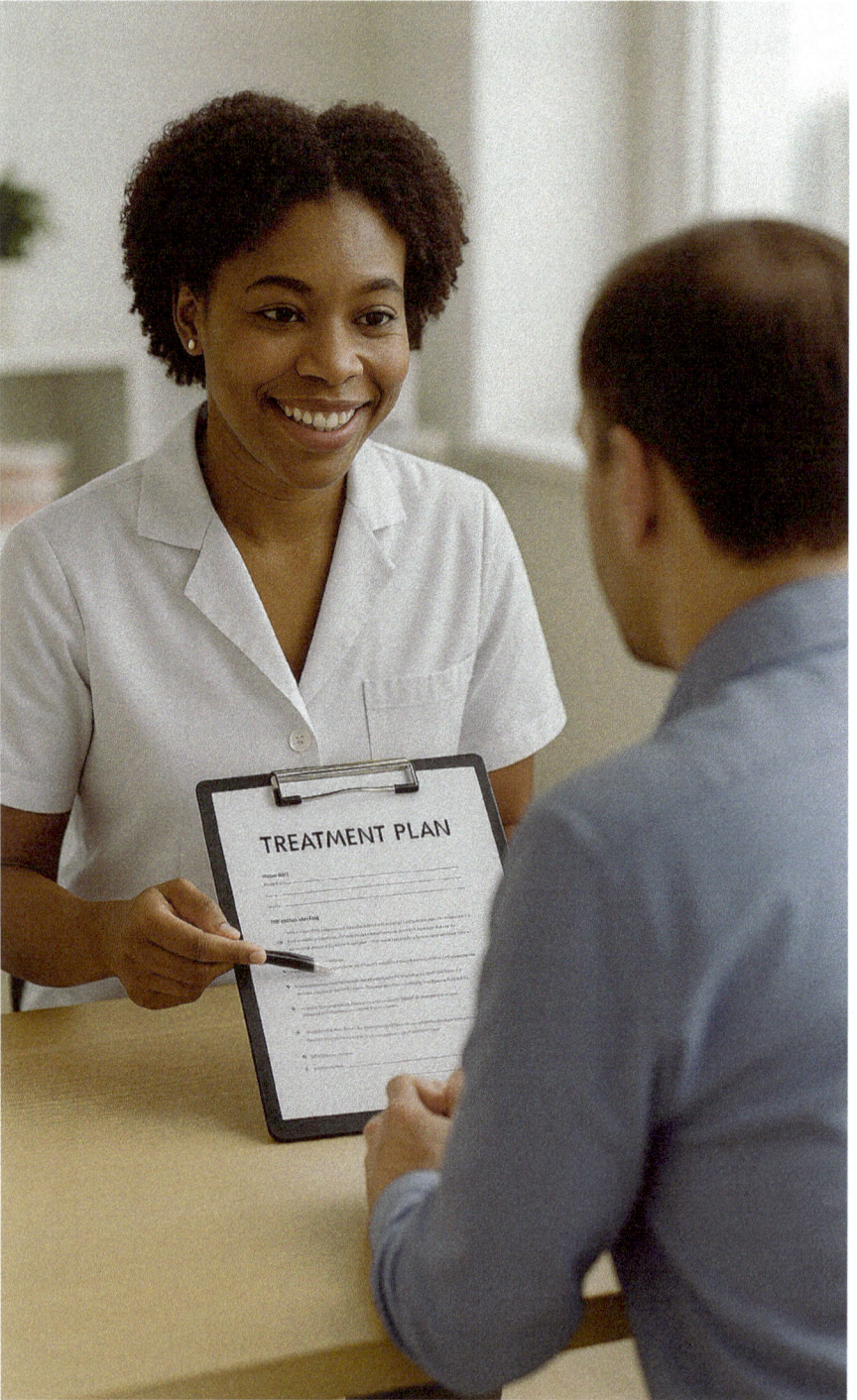

Chapter 9

Successful, Non Stressful Treatment Planning Presentation And Acceptance

The process of having patients accept treatment begins the first moment they sit in your dental chair. It is choreographed and not something thrown out to the patients at the conclusion of the initial exam or other appointment. Honesty, genuine concern and gaining the patient's trust are the key to success.

When people go to a new dentist they have expectations as well as hesitations. What issues will be found on examination? Can they be assured the dentist is honest and above board and qualified in accessing their oral health needs, the cost and future physical discomfort.

I understand these concerns. Over the years, I have observed cases of overselling and under selling of dentistry. In my opinion, both cases are ethically suspect and unprofessional. I understand student loans, office overhead and general cost of living necessities and having the funds to meet needs, but it seems that too much emphasis is often placed on maximizing treatment at all cost. My philosophy has always been "Do unto others" in my approach to treatment planning which is low key and highly successful and almost always accepted. People trust me, come back and seldom leave the practice. Holes in the schedule are rare. I'm not a magician nor do I claim to be the best clinician on earth , but I've learned to sell myself, to communicate my authenticity and compassion, before selling dental services.

Our Goal

At heart, every practitioner wants to see patients accept the care they need. We want to inform the patient of any dental health needs, present possibilities, give options, and have that patient accept treatment. Treatment acceptance keeps our practices healthy and our patients well served. However, not every patient who visits for the first time always returns for follow up care.

Reasons vary and, although I do not know every scenario, patients in the past have told me they came to our office after going elsewhere because of first impressions, general office atmosphere, a sense of being oversold and pressured about treatment giving them a deer in the headlights moment, and even a condescending attitude by the doctor and/ or staff regarding their condition. Patients are not always knowledgeable when it comes to treatment options, elective possibilities and specific treatment rationale, but they are not stupid!

Treatment Needs

Patients practicing good oral hygiene and receiving regular dental care with minimal needed treatment or interested in elective esthetics, ready for an implant or crown, veneers, bleaching or aligners are seldom a worry about returning to your office. Presenting them with a treatment plan at the end of the appointment typically feels natural and stress free. These are non stressful situations for both the doctor and patient, there is no immediate need, and the patient does not feel pressured to make decisions, Then there are those patients with more extensive or urgent needs. These patients are aware they need help, perhaps have gotten into that situation due to fear of the dentist or financial concerns, and are nervous before they come to your office for fear of what you will find and the eventual cost. These are the patients most easily scared away, often from sticker shock. I have never had an issue with this scenario because my goal is to kill them with kindness, compassion and zero pressure. I am seeking long term relationships. If a patient's dentition is in excellent condition, I might say " Mrs. Smith, we have a problem here. You have no cavities or issues requiring attention. How do you expect me to make a living that way? Therefore I am prescribing you drink at least three Mountain Dews a day and brush and floss just twice weekly until your next scheduled recall appointment to see if we can rectify this situation ". They appreciate the compliment and the humor.

In the case of the patients with more immediate needs, it is best to put them at ease and give them a sense of control. Handing them a treatment plan as they leave the office with a cost of three endo treatments, buildups and crowns, two implants and eight composites will scare the heck out of anyone not named Bill Gates. First and foremost, listen to them, let them share their story and concerns and applaud their courage for coming in. The primary goal we aspire to at the end of the appointment is for the patient to feel cared for, sense genuine concern for their problems, have hope, dispel their fears and give them a sense of control going forward concerning future treatment.

As stated before, these people are aware they need help. They often apologize for their condition, are ashamed , may have had bad prior experiences and it has taken a great deal of courage for them to even come for a dental appointment. I've even had people cry on occasion. Our job is to let them know we are happy they made the decision to come, be non judgmental, put them at ease and give them hope and establish trust. I handle it thusly. " Miss Kelly, we have gone over everything and both of us know there are a number of areas for concern, but together we can begin getting your oral health in better condition. Just remember, Rome wasn't built in a day and our first concern is to get your foundation back in good order. When you build a home, a good foundation is most important, and on that same foundation you can build an expensive or inexpensive home. It is up to you. Remember, it is your mouth, your money, your time. We are here to serve you. First, let us get your foundation in order. Then we will discuss options and give reasons for each and you will make the final decision on how to proceed". Oftentimes, there is an audible sigh of relief. I've even had people thank me and give me a hug upon leaving. It is most gratifying. We present them with a first step treatment plan as a starter. This is an opportunity to build trust and a good relationship between doctor and patient before proceeding to the next, more expensive and extensive phase of treatment. These people are appreciative, return for treatment, become loyal patients and refer lots of new people to your practice.

Initial Exam

The initial exam appointment is important in that it sets the stage and our goal should be to give the patient a sense of perceived value and confidence in our abilities and concern for their care. It begins with a cheerful greeting from the hygienist and attentive seating and inquiring if they have any immediate concerns followed by evaluation of the health history, the panoramic and other radiographs as needed, blood pressure and pre doctor charting. In my opinion, no initial exam is complete unless a Pan is taken whether insurance pays for or not. Otherwise, a dentist opens themself up for the possibility of malpractice litigation having missed a number of possible problems that full mouth radiographs fail to show. A panoramic x Ray is also a great teaching tool for the big picture. Use a laser or extended pointer for show and tell.

First Impressions Matter

From my first day in practice I have worn a dress shirt, tie and white clinic jacket. I want there to be no doubt who has just entered the room and to look the professional I am. After a warm greeting and reviewing preliminary hygiene charting and notes I examine radiographs and dentition. I then proceed into teaching mode with the panorex on the monitor "Ms. Jackson, I guess you think I'm looking at your teeth first, but that is the last thing we will be looking at today". I then review the sinuses, comment on any abnormalities , sinusitis or other issues, review the nasal passage openings and may note a deviated septum, examine the TMJ condition, maxillary and mandibular bone for any cysts, abscesses, bone level, impacted teeth, or supernumerary dentition, and retained root tips. I may comment on seeing plaque build up in the carotid arteries at C3 level, and suggest seeing a cardiologist. We review the dentition on the panorex and then full mouth radiographs as necessary to show caries or other concerns. People are blown away, and often say they have never had such an exam at the dental office. We palpate the TMJ, lymph nodes and do an oral cancer exam. There is never any doubt in their minds of the perceived value received and money spent for the appointment.

Patients Are Alert

Remember, during charting the patient is alert and hears dialog between the dentist and hygienist. This gives the doctor a double opportunity to make them aware of the treatment needs. What the doctor says and how they say it is so important. Always use understandable rather than technical language when possible .For instance, "Morgan, we have a large DO cavity (don't say caries) on tooth number four. We need to fix that before it gets any bigger and causes further issues. We also have a large restoration and some fracture lines on tooth number 14 and I suggest a crown to hopefully prevent problems in the future."Hopefully the hygienist has already made them aware using radiographs and the intra oral camera, or you can show it to them at this time. You get the idea.

Show And Tell

In my opinion, every operatory should be equipped with an intraoral camera and a large mounted TV monitor for ease of case viewing. The old adage "a picture is worth 1000 words" holds very much true and an intraoral camera is a great tool when used properly and consistently. It is not expensive technology anymore. I have one in every operatory , but definitely have one in the hygiene room/rooms, and another in at least one treatment room where you will see most of your emergency patients. That room can also be utilized for show and tell in treatment planning presentations.

Team Involvement

The hygienist and the assistants need to use the intra oral camera, models and other teaching tools more. It is worth scheduling additional time for every initial workup exam appointment. There is no excuse for hygienists and assistants not being proficient in their utilization to the maximum each opportunity they get to show large restorations, diminished smiles by old or even new amalgams or showing patients they could benefit from bleaching or aligners or traditional ortho and anything else that's pertinent..

We never wish to be perceived as pushy but, if a service can enhance the patient's feeling of well being and overall oral health, whether tooth whitening or alignment, crowns, veneers, Botox or other services we should be proclaiming these options from the rooftops. The entire team needs to be on the same page with this. Every operatory should have its own bleaching shade guide available, handouts and models on aligners, veneers, crowns, implants and other offered treatments and every hygienist and assistant when alone with a patient should evaluate potential need and mention it subtly. For instance " Miss Smith, you have such nice teeth. I wonder if you have ever considered having them whitened a bit? If you don't mind, I like to see what shade you are. My shade guide shows you're an A 3 shade currently and you can probably lighten them a couple shades above that" and show them the improvement after whitening. or " Mrs. Jones, your teeth are so nice but have you ever considered having them straightened? If so, it can normally be done nowadays without all the brackets and wires. The doctor can tell you if that would work in your case"

Consider what additional income two bleaching or two alignment cases a week for 48 weeks a year would mean for your yearly income. This can be accomplished subtly, without pressure, and is a genuine service to patients and their feelings of self worth and increased self confidence. Every patient should at least be aware of what is available

Treatment Plan Presentation

When presenting any treatment plan, always be flexible and, when possible, offer alternative treatments. Review findings. Use visual aids like models, videos and radiographs, give long term benefits and risks of not doing a procedure and use non technical language. Whoever presents the treatment plan should STRESS that the patient ask questions if they have any. Any improvement is better than no improvement at all but , in most cases, the long term prognosis at a greater cost wins out when the patient is made aware of negative potential issues down the road of interim treatment. For the more difficult and /or extensive cases present the treatment plan in more manageable phases so as to get the patient's dental foundation in good order before proceeding and to provide time for relationship building before advancing to future stages of treatment. Any patient overly concerned about cost can be put at ease by being informed, when possible, that full treatment can be done over time and that financing plans are available.

These are simply suggestions that, if utilized properly, can enhance patient treatment plan acceptance in a non stressful manner and improve return for treatment numbers . Obviously everyone will not follow through with suggested treatment but, if the patient feels more in control of their treatment as far as timeframe, decision making and finances ,they are more likely to accept treatment. The goal is to have them leave your office informed, impressed and trusting in the next step.

Reflection And Practice

- Take note of the previous instructions and evaluate how to improve current treatment plan presentations
- Review the past 90 days treatment plan acceptance rates and patient return for services after initial exam appointments and , as a team, discuss possible scenarios for improvement.

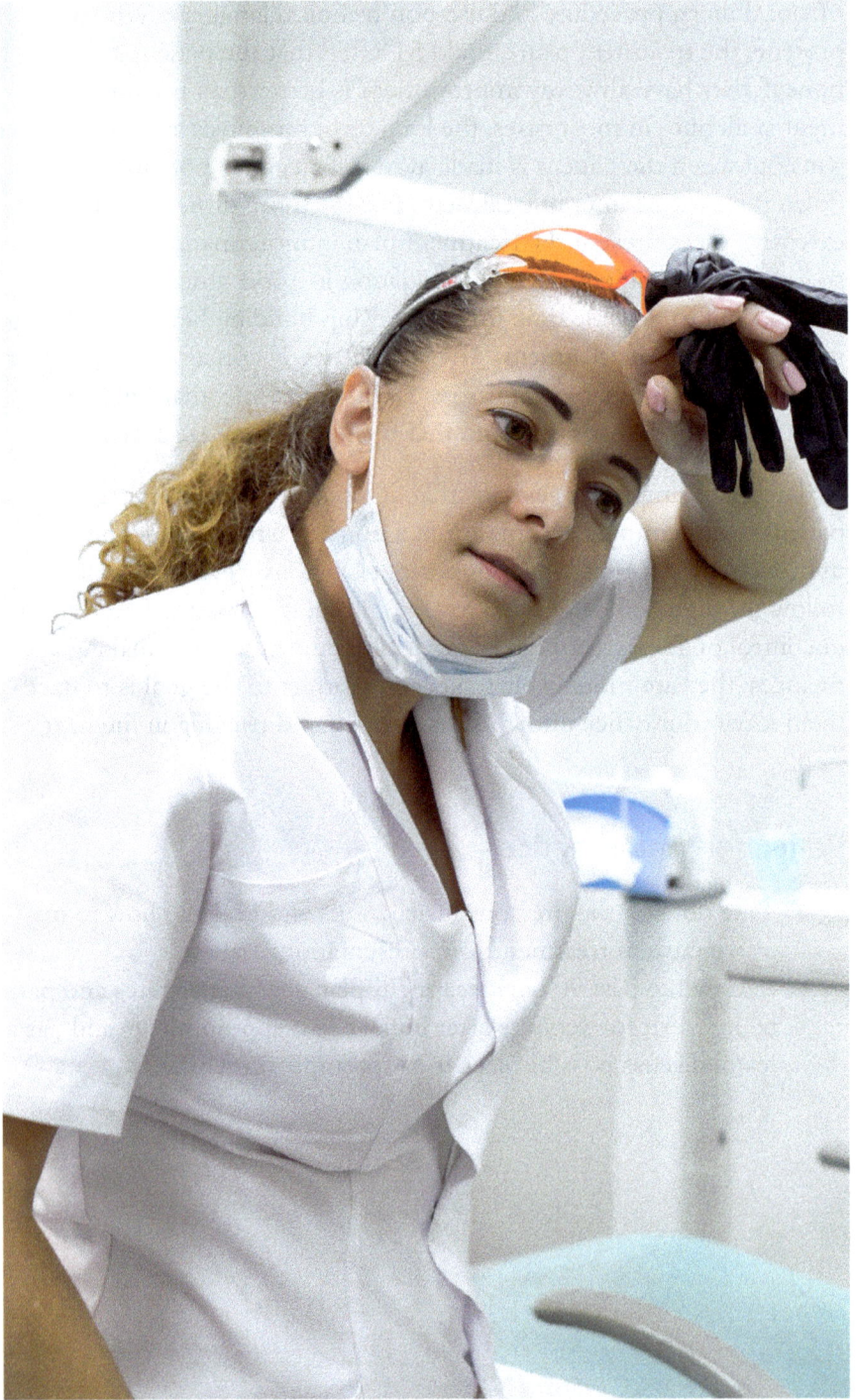

Chapter 10

Understanding And Coping With Dental Practice Stress

The day began poorly. One assistant called in sick, an operatory unit malfunctioned, and an unexpected complication during my first procedure put me 30 minutes behind schedule. My next patient required an endo and buildup, forcing us to reschedule the following appointment just to regain some control. Ever had a day like that? Hopefully they are a rarity.

Dentistry can indeed be stressful. Trying to please patients, busy schedules, managing staff, and running a business when combined with family pressures and other personal issues can seem an overwhelming burden at times. While we can't always control unexpected stressful situations, we can—and should—identify the primary stressors in our lives and make intentional efforts to reduce their impact. Circumstances do not have to control us. Some stress is inevitable, but suffering is optional. We must learn to master our responses, accept that perfection is unrealistic, and be more in control of our lives. That is the key. Allowing circumstances to always control us rather than learning to control circumstances is a certain recipe for disillusionment, unfulfillment, and eventual burnout. According to the ADA 2021 Well-Being Survey, the majority of dentists reported feeling major stressors in life and career. Younger dentists and female dentists are disproportionately affected by mental and emotional health concerns. Thirty-nine percent of all dentists feel hopeless about their future, 23 percent report moderate to severe depression, 25 percent emotional exhaustion, and 13 percent severe burnout. Eighty-four percent of practitioners report pain with lower back, neck, shoulders, and hands while working, and some hearing loss is common.

Not every dentist faces ongoing stress at an extreme level. For some it is a non-issue! Each person handles stress differently. What's overwhelming for one might barely register for another. It is not that one is strong and another weak. They may be equal in knowledge and skills but different in acclimation ability. Still, for many dentists, practice stress is a major concern and affects quality of life and happiness. That is why it is important for state and national associations to provide a readily available support system and to make every member aware of how to access help immediately in time of need.

Common Stress-Inducing Traits in Dentists:

Many personality traits such as conscientiousness, focus, determination, competitiveness, and others that were necessary and essential in our effort to get into dental school can also make us more susceptible to stress and burnout later in life. See if any of these apply in your own case:

1. Conscientiousness
2. Compulsive attention to detail
3. Tendency to control emotional expression
4. Delayed gratification
5. Workaholic tendencies
6. Competitiveness
7. Goal-oriented
8. Need for order and clear information
9. Preference for solitude away from practice
10. Hesitance to share personal concerns
11. Dependence on professional success for self-esteem

Coping Strategies for Managing Stress

1. Accept that stress can never be totally eliminated, only minimized. We must learn to control our environment rather than always letting it control us.

2. Identify key stressors and act decisively to address them.

3. Create realistic 3-to-5-year plans covering your professional, financial, and personal goals.

4. Prioritize your life—learn to balance practice, family, economic, and spiritual aspects. Leave practice issues at the office and concentrate on quality family time at home.

5. Improve your working environment, and attempt to be less isolated away from the office.

6. Schedule sacred time off, including regular short mini-breaks.

7. Practice positive self-talk. Concentrate on positive aspects of your life rather than dwelling on the negative.

8. Do your best, acknowledging that you can't please everyone. Expecting perfection is unrealistic.

9. Eliminate or minimize negative influences—people, places, things, or habits.

10. Learn relaxation techniques and practice regularly.

11. Make efforts to improve sleep patterns.

12. Focus on better nutrition and physical health.

13. Consider a spiritual approach to life.

14. Plan long-term but enjoy the present moment.

15. Regularly reward yourself for both small and large successes.

16. Overcome fear factors that tend to control our lives. Most never materialize.

17. Never apologize or feel guilty for success.

18. Consider hiring an associate if your practice workload becomes too demanding.

19. Build a support system through organized dentistry or close peers.

20. Seek professional help early, without shame or hesitation.

Insights from Our National Dental Stress Survey:

We mailed a comprehensive stress survey to 5,000 dentists nation-wide, receiving an overwhelming response. In truth, very little attention has been directed to this area of concern over the years. Dentistry uniquely involves intimate patient care—performing sensitive proce-dures while managing patient anxiety and expectations daily. Dentists are never expected to make mistakes. Tell me of another profession where we work all day inches from someone's face, take a needle and poke as painlessly as possible into their very personal orifice, all the while wanting them to like us. On top of that, they pay us to inflict such an intimate invasion of privacy and dislike the loss of finances as much as the needle. Oddly as it may seem, we are most often the re-cipients of our patients' love and respect, and dentistry as a profession is held in high esteem. In addition, we also face pressures daily in our practice dealing with diverse personalities among staff and patients, equipment issues, scheduling conflicts, and financial concerns.

Stress Is Not Always Negative

Some level of stress can often energize and motivate! Yet when stress becomes overwhelming, it turns harmful. Much of the stress dentists experience arises from unrealistic expectations. We are imper-fect humans working on imperfect patients using imperfect materials, yet too often expecting perfection. We are stoic individuals perform-ing heroic deeds daily in saving the dentition of those who place their trust in us. Most literature and CE courses are upbeat and seldom acknowledge stress factors in our profession, and many dentists are hesitant to hint of anything untoward in their life. When did you last attend a course or meeting where participants openly shared problems or tensions in their lives? Few admit to being being too busy or not busy enough, unfulfilled dreams, their back or neck hurts all the time, their hygienist is pregnant and wants three months off after the baby is born, or the receptionist just quit without notice. Most dentists have no one to share concerns or discuss plans except their poor spouse who has heard it all before. When stress becomes overwhelming, many are reluctant to seek support when needed, thus intensifying the situation. Iron men and women, we often tend to protect our privacy while holding things inside, hesitant to reach out for help until it is too late.

Dental Stressors Listed in Our Survey:

- Running behind schedule levels
- Not enough time each day self
- I must do things myself if I want them done correctly
- Need for and expectations of perfection
- Difficulty saying "NO" without feeling guilt
- Constant time pressure control
- Desire to always avoid conflict
- Financial concerns
- Fear of failure
- Patients not appreciative of what I do
- Never feel rested
- Staff relationships/issues
- People fail to listen well
- Worry about others' opinions
- High concentration
- High expectations of
- Fear of mistakes
- Anxious patients
- Not where I want to be in life
- Need to always be in
- Too many patients
- Too few patients
- Dental emergencies
- Changes in technology
- Practice isolation
- Repetitive nature of work
- Sense of confinement
- Career doubts

Survey respondents were asked to assign a number from one to four to each of the stressors listed, with four being extremely stressful. A number of stressors were close in final calculations, but the survey top ten were as follows:

1. Running behind schedule
2. Constant time pressure
3. High expectations of self
4. Dissatisfied, ungrateful patients
5. Anxious patients
6. Expectation of clinical perfection
7. Fear of failure
8. Desire to avoid conflict
9. Staff relationship issues
10. Feeling behind in life's goals

About half of these stressors stem directly from staff or patient interactions—often due to inadequate leadership on the part of the dentist—while the rest emerge from self-imposed, often unrealistic, expectations. Interestingly, clinical mistakes, malpractice fears, and technological changes ranked lower, indicating dentists generally feel confident in these areas.

Still, in our survey, 38% reported experiencing burnout symptoms at some point. Comments ranged from highly optimistic to deeply negative and hopeless. If stress negatively impacts your professional or personal life, actively seek ways to mitigate it through lifestyle adjustments, professional counseling, improved planning, good leadership, and realistic expectations.

One respondent summarized the stress perfectly: "Running a dental practice sometimes feels like driving a car while someone else keeps tugging at the wheel." Reinhold Niebuhr offered timeless wisdom: "God, grant me the serenity to accept the things I cannot change, courage to change the things I can, and wisdom to know the difference."

Reflection And Practice

- Review the list of survey questions and list your top 10 life stressors.
- Consider if they are realistic or self determined
- Pick two to begin working on. Start slow so as not to become discouraged
- Review personal and professional priorities and list circumstances in your life that may be interfering.

Chapter 11

Stressless Staff

The Daily Toll of Staff Stress

Although staff-related stress might not top national surveys for practice stressors, when it does surface, it often cuts deeper and seems more personal than other issues .You face it daily, and it can feel relentless. Leadership is critical here—if you need a refresher, revisit the chapter on leadership. While other top stressors are explored in a separate chapter, staff stress deserves its own deep dive, because it's frequently more emotionally fraught than scheduling or financial concerns.

Every dentist, at some point, deals with staff-induced stress. In the best scenarios, it's short-lived or easily addressed. But if left unchecked, it becomes a constant thorn in your side, draining your energy and enjoyment of the profession. You do not look forward to going to the office in the morning. Complete elimination of staff stress is impossible over the lifetime of a practice, but you can minimize its frequency and impact by being proactive, planning ahead, hiring wisely and exercising strong leadership. Being more in control of situations rather than allowing situations to control us is the key. Harmony among staff is the fertile soil from which success booms. Tend the roots of cooperation and your practice will flourish in peace.

Solving the "Staff Stress" Puzzle

People are inherently different—personalities, work ethics, and communication styles vary widely. With a small team, it's easier to remain on the same page. With a larger team a lot more factors are introduced and must be dealt with. A dentist can control some of this through strategic hiring practices, a topic covered in "Reducing Stress and Minimizing Mistakes in the Hiring Process." Yet, in most situations, the staff is already in place and well entrenched. Sometimes the solution involves removing one or two "troublemakers," restructuring roles, or applying new policies that initially may be unpopular but ultimately restore order.

It's rare that an entire staff is irreparably broken. Often, it just needs realignment or "tweaking" to straighten out issues before they become insurmountable.

Factors Affecting Turnover And Dysfunction

While strong, well respected leadership is absolutely mandatory, other factors should be considered.

1. Office Resources & Efficiency

   o Is there enough workspace, equipment, and supplies to meet daily demands?
   o Are operatories similarly equipped with supplies,X-rays, cameras,monitors and other equipment considering procedures performed
   o Is your schedule out of control
   o For continuity, is there at least one designated person for ordering supplies in each area (front office, hygiene, restorative rooms), and do you have a system (e.g., a "Supplies Needed" list) to keep track?

2. Team Size & Scheduling

   o Is the team too large or too small for the types of procedures and volume of patients? Excessive workload is a major stressor.
   o Are you overstaffed, leading to idle time , friction and increased overhead or understaffed, causing stress and chaos?
   o Are your patients mostly large-case or small-case? Socio-economic status might influence time required for treatment

planning presentations or financial arrangements.
- Flexibility factor; how far scheduled out?
- Number of hygienists and doctors

3. State & Legal Constraints

- Do state laws limit hygiene exams or assistant expanded duties, causing bottlenecks?
- Does the practice schedule allow hygienists and assistants to work efficiently within legal parameters?

4. Advances in Equipment & Materials

- Are you keeping current with newer materials, delivery systems, software or other time-saving technologies?

5. Leadership Strength

- Are you practicing decisive leadership? Strong leaders proactively address problems, communicate clearly, and set expectations.

Key Reminder: Continuity reduces stress at every level. When the team knows what to expect—procedurally and interpersonally—they can work more confidently and collaboratively. A staff becomes stressed when equipment and supplies must be shared between rooms or there are inadequate operatories for the patient load. The schedule suffers, patients complain and tension increases. The top two stressors in our national stress survey were running behind schedule and constant time pressure. These areas are significantly impacted when a schedule is not running smoothly.

Morning Meetings: Start the Day Right

As previously discussed, daily "morning huddles" or staff meetings are essential to give everyone a head start:

- Offer a genuine welcome: Attitude is contagious! A positive tone from the outset helps everyone feel motivated. Have a designated meeting facilitator to keep the meeting running smoothly and on schedule. Done correctly a meeting should run no more than 15-20 minutes

- Review the current day's (and sometimes previous or next day's) schedule
- Discuss open time slots, emergency blocks, key procedures, lab cases, financial matters , treatment follow ups and any challenging patients.

- Address medical alerts, unconfirmed appointments, and follow-up care. This brief gathering fosters team readiness, reduces surprises, and boosts morale.

Reducing Stress in Specific Areas

Front Office

- Own the Schedule: Implement clear policies on emergencies, no-shows, and last-minute cancellations. Adhere to policies.
- Support Staff: Be willing to confront issues as needed rather than put the burden on front office staff . That is the dentist's responsibility!
- Delegate Well. Ensure you've got the right person in the right position. Cross-train for backup support and trust their ability to do the job when adequately trained.
- Trust & Encouragement: Empower staff to take initiative. Acknowledge good work publicly.
- Adequate Tools: Provide enough computer stations,user friendly software and supplies

Dental Assistants

- Training & Resources: Have adequate numbers for schedule support. Make sure they are well-trained and have the materials they need in each operatory'
- Refrain from working in additional procedures or changing procedures midstream
- Give clear, concise instructions. Address assistants in respectful manner at all times
- Attempt to avoid running behind or over into lunch or past quitting time as much as possible

Hygiene Department

- Reasonable Scheduling: Allow sufficient time for hygiene appointments to maintain a calm workflow.
- Early exams: If possible, the dentist should check hygiene patients early to avoid backups.
- Autonomy & Collaboration: Increased autonomy in decision making; procedures, supplies, equipment, hygiene or front office scheduling
- Team Mindset: Watch out for "prima donna" behavior—everyone's role is essential.
- Compensation: Decide on salary or production-based pay, ensuring fairness and clarity.
- Consider a Hygiene Assistant: In a busy practice, an assistant can significantly reduce hygienist stress and help keep on schedule. That individual is also available as needed in other cases schedule permits.

Providing continuing education opportunities for staff elevates their sense of professionalism and worth to the practice. Cross training helps staff appreciate what is involved in and the importance of co- workers' role in ensuring the practice runs smoothly and ultimate practice success.

Addressing "Problem Patients"

Policies exist for a reason. Enforce them consistently. This includes:

- Dress code, no-show, or late-arrival policies.
- Financial agreements and respect for staff.
- Dismissing consistently non-compliant or abusive patients can be a relief for the entire team.

The crucial point: Always backup your staff. They need to know you stand with them when dealing with difficult individuals or in difficult situations

Handling Grievances

No one enjoys confrontation. I certainly do not but there are times when an employee needs to be counseled , a situation needs to be addressed for the health of the practice or a conflict arises between doctor and team member or team members. Do not procrastinate and counsel earlier than later. Sadly the issue will not resolve itself. Counsel from a position of strength. Have your facts to present. Refer to the policy and job description manuals. If it becomes evident the employee is hesitant or unwilling to make the necessary effort to alleviate the situation, decide if you really wish to retain their services. I refer to this as the " cancer scenario" because it is better to remove the offending part than to allow it to grow worse and destroy office harmony. Document, document, document!!!! Never fear an increase in unemployment insurance when the health of the practice is at stake. If everything is documented , including previous counseling sessions, this should not be an issue since you have the facts to back you up.

Employee Counseling And Grievance Procedures

- **Act Swiftly:** Don't procrastinate. Confront issues early from a position of strength and preparation.
- **Document Everything:** Keep clear records of incidents, verbal or written warnings, and steps taken. Have a counselled individual sign the record of the counseling session..
- **Refer to Policies:** Use your office policy and job description manuals to guide discussions.
- **Decision Point:** If an employee resists improvement or refuses to align with practice values, it may be time for termination. Think of it like removing a small "cancer" before it spreads

Between Staff

- **Clear Protocol:** Grievance procedures should be in the policy manual, reviewed annually.
- **Staff vs. Staff:** Encourage them to resolve minor conflicts one-on-one first; if that fails, intervene.

- **Gather Facts Individually:** Meet each person separately, then together, once you understand the situation better give advice as to possible solutions.
- **Encourage** their trying to understand each other's perspective and discuss possible solutions
- **Document** and have both parties sign
- **Firm Resolutions:** If problems persist, make th.e hard choice- sometimes letting an employee go is best for team morale. If desiring to retain both parties consider a mediator.
- **Unification followup:** After resolution of issue, explain to staff, if desired, as much as is appropriate and move on.

Doctor vs Staff member

- **Private Conversation:** Discuss issues confidentially without public embarrassment
- **Listen:** Hear employees perspective and balance it with known facts, office policy manual and job descriptions.
- **Accountability:** Own your mistakes but do not shoulder blame where there is none.
- **Explore** possible solutions from each parties perspective
- **Outcome:** If a workable outcome cannot be reached, termination might be necessary

Points to Ponder

1. Limit personal phone calls for both doctor and staff.
2. Delegate effectively and avoid micromanaging.
3. Educate team members on the importance of each role to practice success; front office, assisting, and hygiene.
4. Model teamwork yourself.
5. Stay on schedule to reduce everyone's stress.
6. Be proactive when problems arise—early action is key.
7. Embrace positive change.
8. Prepare staff for changes by explaining the benefits beforehand.

Staff resistance is offset by understanding the purpose and ultimate benefits to the practice.

9. Review salaries regularly; consider bonuses, perks, and flexible schedules.

10. Show genuine appreciation often.

11. Remember your staff has a life outside the office—show concern.

12. Counsel or discipline in private, preserving employee dignity.

13. Encourage patient responsibility.

14. Publicly affirm staff competence to patients ("Patty did an excellent job with your temporary…").

15. Uniforms and name tags can boost professional identity.

16. Share positive patient feedback with the entire team.

17. If there's open time in the schedule, use it productively (cleaning, stocking, lab work) rather than complaining.

18. Post office purpose and philosophy statements in staff areas as daily reminders.

19. Focus on procedures you're best at and enjoy for a more fulfilling practice experience.

20. Demand responsibility from patients

A Note on Team Building: Group Trips

Every year, I send my entire staff on a three-night, two-day trip. It doesn't have to be Paris or Rome—somewhere drivable and affordable is fine. Because our practice is in North Georgia, destinations like Hilton Head, Gatlinburg, or Charleston work well. Staff members share rooms with co-workers from different departments (e.g., front office paired with hygiene). Over time, these short getaways have forged deeper relationships and a greater sense of unity. Money spent on team building always pays you back in loyalty and cohesiveness. Once a month a longer lunch break is scheduled for the team to go to lunch and periodically I excuse myself because they have a better time together bonding when the DOCTOR ISN'T AROUND.. Just a fact!

The Nuclear Option: Starting Over

These steps won't cover every scenario, but they offer a strong foundation for minimizing staff-related stress. Sometimes though a practice is so dysfunctional that the best move is to start fresh. Yes, firing people en masse, closing for a week to hire and train new staff, and dealing with short-term production losses. can be scary. You must plan ahead and have replacements in mind but if it means safeguarding your sanity and securing your practice's future, it's worth it. Often, you'll recover far quicker and never look back.

Trust me—living with constant chaos is far more stressful than making a bold move toward restoring harmony.

Contact Dr. Stough at gstoughdmd@gmail.com

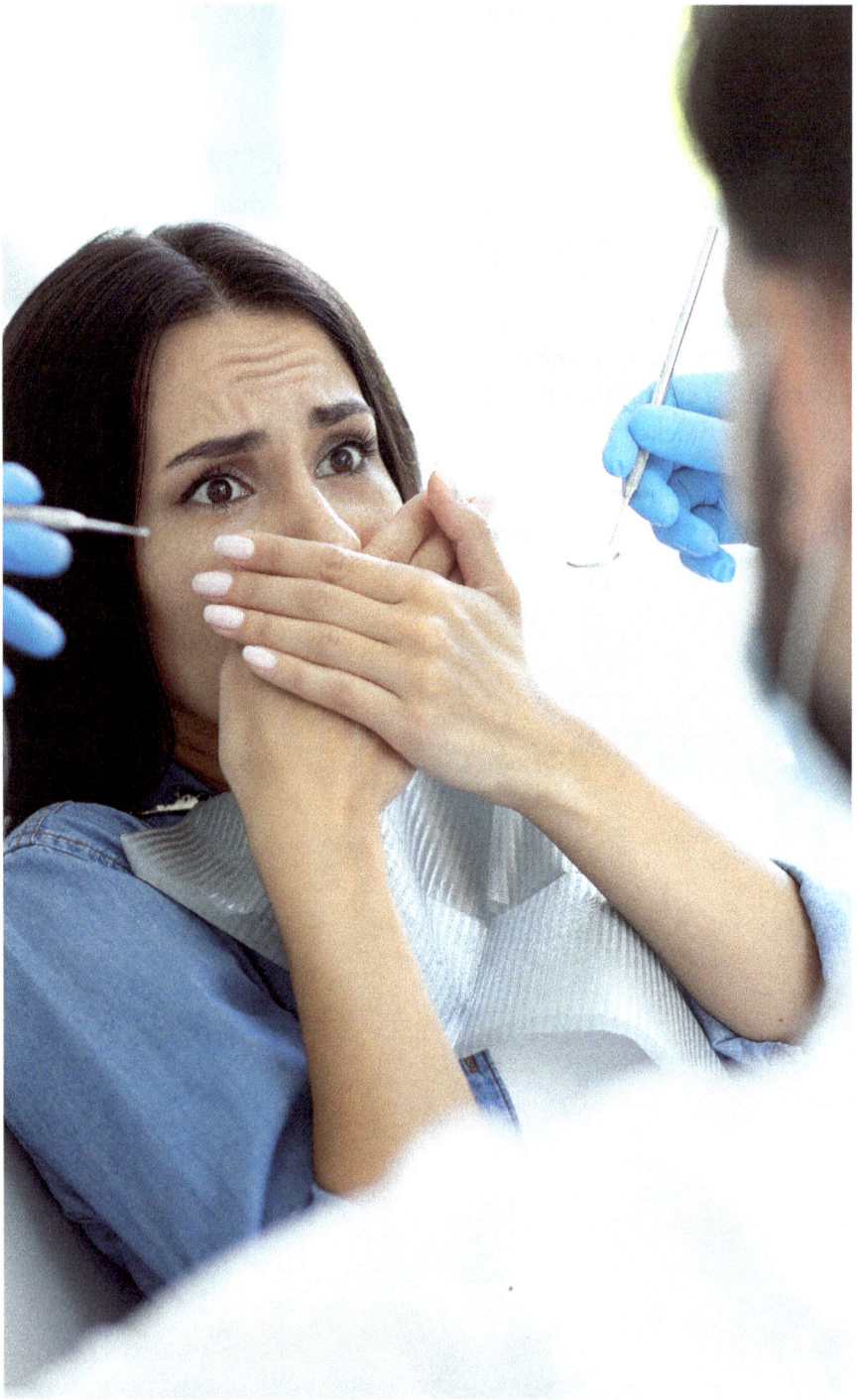

Chapter 12

Top Ten Survey Stressors Reviewed

Each reader has their own personal list which might have little resemblance to our survey's top ten. Therefore each must do his/her own personal evaluation in determining what steps need to be taken to lessen stressors in their own lives. Still, reviewing our survey's top ten will serve as a template going forward.

Running Behind Schedule

1. Poorly planned or no morning meetings
2. Too little time scheduled for procedures.
3. Not taking hygiene schedule into consideration and double booking procedures
4. Scheduler's evaluation of real versus perceived emergencies.
5. Too few or poorly trained staff
6. Failure to delegate adequately
7. Insufficient operatories, equipment, supplies
8. Excessive time checking hygiene
9. Inserting additional, unplanned procedures in scheduled time
10. Accommodating patients late for appointments
11. Receiving/ making phone calls that can be attended to in down time

12. Hire an associate if too busy

Constant Time Pressures

1. Includes many areas under Running Behind Schedule
2. Family and community commitment obligations
3. Always conforming to patient's schedules rather than having others conform to yours
4. Difficulty or unwillingness saying NO when warranted
5. Attempting to be all things to all people

High Expectations Of Self

1. Often unrealistic. Whose expectations are you trying to live up to?
2. Do not simply equate success with production and collection numbers. Resist comparing to others
3. Know limitations. Dwell on your strengths rather than perceived shortcoming
4. One cannot expect to do all procedures well at all times under every circumstance. Simply do your best which, in reality, is probably better than many others. You are probably more successful, competitive and better in comparison than you are aware.

Dissatisfied, Ungrateful Patients

1. Impossible to satisfy all the people all the time
2. Do not attempt procedures beyond your expertise
3. Failure to perform each procedure to the best of your ability. Attempting short cuts.
4. Inadequate pre-op/post op instructions
5. Inform then perform. Adequately explain procedures, limitations, probable scenarios, time required and finances
6. Staff considerations

    a.   Poor telephone skills/manners

    b.   Perceived lack of sympathy/ empathy for patients situation

    c.   Poor knowledge/ handling of real versus perceived emergencies

7. Patients unrealistic expectations

    a.   Give worse case scenario up front

    b.   Bonding vs veneer vs crown longevity

    c.   Stress achievable esthetics of various treatments. You cannot turn a sow's ear into a silk purse

    d.   Role of good oral hygiene in long term success- patient responsibility

8. Put blame on the patient's condition where it belongs; on the patient!!! Do not assume responsibility. If there is any possibility of pain after treatment, give the patient the worse case scenario and scare them a little. If they have no post treatment pain they will think you are a hero. If they do experience pain they will remember you informed them of the possibility and not hold you responsible

9. Patients lack knowledge /appreciation of what is involved in the delivery of treatment and perceived value. Educate them.

10. Expectations of Cadillac dentistry at Chevrolet prices.

11. Never say permanent

12. Explain in non medical terms so patients understands more clearly

13. No politics, religion or personal beliefs expressed during patient visit, Neutrality!!

14. Continually running behind schedule. If more than 20 minutes late, give patients a 5% discount off the day's treatment cost. It is an incentive to keep us on schedule andbdiffuses patient irritation of having to wait.
    Great referral tool!

Anxious Patients

1. Acceptance: certain percentage of people will be anxious no matter what the dentist or hygienist(s) do

2. Do not assume responsibility or incur guilt for patients anxious state

3. Refer when it is in your and the patient's best interest. Wise decision!!

4. Fear of injections, sounds, smells. Go slowly !!! Attempt infiltration rather than block when possible. .

5. Tone of voice, gentle caring attitude of doctor and staff and explaining the day's procedure has positive results. Give the patient some control:
   "Mr Jones, raise your left hand if you experience discomfort, need to swallow or just need to rest a moment."
   Patients love it!!!!

6. Oral or IV sedation

Fear Of Failure

1. Is normal within reason. Often result of low self esteem. Finances, business competition, schedule demands and possible loss of relevance and fear of rejection are just some common fears.

2. Some level of fear may temper our decision making and guide us conservatively in financial or other matters but can also hold us back ,stifle growth, induce stagnation, prolong ability to retire, growth of the practice and ability to reach out and take life by the horns. Most fears are unrealistic. It undermines our sense of well being,

3. Unrealistic expectations. Set realistic goals and plan a step by step strategy that is controllable and celebrate each success along the way which builds confidence.

4. Seek a support network for advise, guidance and encouragement

Avoidence Of Conflict

1. No one likes conflict but some conflict is unavoidable.
   Some people are conflict addicts. I call it a BULLY PERSON-ALITY'. If they make you unhappy then they are in control. It makes them happy at your expense. Simply avoid them as much as possible or fire them and let them bully some other poor dentist

2. Review " Dissatisfied, ungrateful patients"

3. Establish parameters, rules and expectations and expect people to follow them.
   Institute select purging of patients, staff and others as required to reduce current and future conflict issues

4. The best defense is often a good offense. Evaluate the situation and act. Meet conflict head on.' Do we have a problem ?" Confront the bully's personality head on.

5. If you run away from it today it will be even worse tomorrow. Do not shoulder others' guilt or blame. Place blame where blame belongs

Expectations And Need For Perfection

1. A desire for perfection is understandable and admirable and can motivate us to perform at a high level and deliver excellent results. The need for and expectations is unreasonable and unhealthy.

2. It connotes an unrealistic perception of our abilities, patient compliance or the world as a whole. Rooted in personal insecurity.

3. Promotes a self defeating image that we are less than a good dentist, parent, lover (add your own list) if every procedure is not successful, every patient not satisfied, our spouse isn't always happy or our children don't live up to expectations.

4. Extension of the unrealistic dental school mentality into the REAL world

5. Constantly dwelling upon real or perceived shortcomings leaves one stressed and unfulfilled.

6. Can only be overcome by setting realistic goals, accepting personal limitations and personal expectations. Expecting and needing perfection can create the need to live up to others financially, socially and personally and dwelling on our place within the dental pecking order which is unnecessary and unproductive

Staff Related Stress

Read the chapter entitled Stress-Less Staff

Not Where I Want To Be In Life

1. Lack of leadership and control over professional and personal life issues and priorities.

2. Big Hat, No Cattle financial lifestyle; Living above one's means.

3. Poor business administration

4. Unrealistic expectations

5. No 3-5 years plans in place

6. Constant comparisons to others

7. Bad habits and lack of motivation.

8. Making excuses and blaming other for our lack of success

9. Poor social and communication skills

10. Procrastinating. Fear of failure holding us back. Locked into a comfort zone.
    Read the book " WHO MOVED MY CHEESE".

Examine those stressors in this group that may apply to you and your practice situation and attempt to make changes as necessary. Address additional stressors in your life and focus on making needed changes. Seek help if needed. The problem(s) will not rectify themselves but must be addressed for the sake of current and future personal happiness and satisfaction.

Chapter 13

Practice Transition

I am not a practice transition specialist and strongly recommend consulting one when the time comes but in this chapter I want to at least offer some practical insights to help prepare for a smoother path into retirement whether in 5 years, 20 years or beyond. Practice transitions can be complex and the more moving parts involved the greater chance of things going wrong. My philosophy is to keep things as simple and straightforward as possible.

Start Planning Early

It is best to get started planning for retirement early. Ideally that would mean in your first year in practice but it is never too late until it is too late. Contribute whatever possible, no matter how small an amount, to a 401K, IRA or Roth plan. Get into the habit early! Unfortunately too many professionals delay. They tell themselves they will start " someday" once they feel more financially secure. Here's the problem; life rarely unfolds according to plan. You may find yourself trying to keep up with the Joneses (don't), raising, educating and marrying off children (they're wonderful but expensive) , facing unexpected health, home repair or family emergency issues or going through a divorce which quickly turns your 401 K into a 200.5 K. The bottom line; you really cannot afford to wait any longer. Start where you are. It is never too early or too late to seek professional financial advice.

Debt Reduction

Make it a priority to reduce debt early. Few things are more satisfying and elicit a greater sense of freedom than when making that final payment on a loan. It is an exhilarating milestone that opens the door to countless future opportunities. Even a small addition to the principal of a monthly loan payment can save thousands in interest in the long run. Refrain from the " Big Hat,NO Cattle" lifestyle. In other words, do not live above your means to project success. Why do you need to impress others anyway? Stay clear of get rich schemes. If you do, make sure you know what you are doing and that anyone you are involved with has the knowledge and as much to lose as you do if things go south, You are not a bank! They most often lead to disappointment and financial loss or worse. Instead , focus your energy on building a strong, successful practice and personal/professional lifestyle- your most reliable path to long term security.

Transition Strategies

There are many retirement planning scenarios, including associate to partners to buyer, associate to buyer, mergers, selling and walking away or the one I prefer which is hiring an associate to whom you sell and continue working in the practice for a period of time after sale. In my opinion, all the options are fraught with potential negative issues, even the last one but which, if done properly, is the smoothest transition over the shortest period of time, least emotionally taxing, and offers the greatest financial advantages. The more parts one puts into the equation, the more things that can go wrong. Your goal should be to maximize your practice sales potential with greater profit and pad your retirement account. Some financial advisors say not to factor practice sale into your long term retirement plans and to be able to have a firm financial foundation otherwise. I agree but, unless you die, become suddenly disabled, let the practice go to heck towards the end or ruin your reputation, the proceeds from a practice sale can be considerable and provide significant future financial security.

By implementing and enacting a well structured sales plan and maintaining the practice value a practice sale can be a golden egg.

Sell And Skidaddle

Selling one's practice and walking away might seem like a clean break but it is rarely the most financially rewarding option. In doing so a dentist risks not realizing the full value of everything they have worked so hard to build. The dentist is not simply leaving money on the table but is also missing an opportunity to significantly enhance their retirement account. With consistent focus on maintaining and growing your practice's worth in your final years this asset can become your most powerful wealth- building tool. It is essential to have a strong financial foundation outside of one's practice but, unless something goes seriously wrong, e.g. death, disability, substance abuse,neglect or damaged reputation , a well planned, well executed exit strategy can unlock extraordinary value. Handled wisely, your practice isn't just a business- it's the engine that can drive a far more secure and abundant retirement.

Associate To Buy-In To Buy-Out Model

This model is often used and can offer the older doctor-owner a sense of security but it comes with a long list of considerations that must be carefully addressed. For starters you must find the right person because there are long term considerations involved. Besides the simpler things like roles, compensation, benefits, various covenants and files security if the relationship does not work out one must put in place a potential timeline for both a buy-in and eventually buy-out agreement. How about long term compatibility. What happens if either dentist becomes disabled or dies. Is the associate or partner obligated to purchase the practice or simply have the right of first refusal? How about real estate and how the practice is to be valued at time of sale or other financial obligations? What happens to retirement accounts and/ or profit sharing plans?. These are only a few of the important questions.

Mergers

If considering a merger the situation can become even more nuanced. Is the merger between two dentists of close to similar age, a rarity, or is a younger doctor joining forces with/purchasing the practice of an older practitioner to form a new, larger entity. The distinction is not slight. In some cases one doctor may sell their practice entirely in order to smoothly transition into retirement, combine practices in one locale and stay on as an associate for a period of time or practitioners could combine in equal partnership and share ownership. Either scenario can be a complex process with various legal, financial and operational aspects but it can also be a strategic move to integrate patients into a larger, more comprehensive operation. While ideally it sounds like a good idea there are many things to consider beforehand. The value of each practice must be determined as well as a combined practice value and future office location and real estate involved. Then there is the issue with staff retention, health and retirement plans and benefits, allocation of future revenue and expenses, management style and contingency planning for the sudden departure of either dentist. This can be a cultural challenge posing challenges in terms of practice philosophy, morale and patient satisfaction. Dentists, like most business owners, can get rather set in their ways, fall into the ' old dog, new tricks' mentality and understanding and cooperation are a must if success is to be achieved. Like any business decision, due diligence and exploring any and all potential pitfalls is absolutely a must. Compatibility is crucial!

A Better Way

The option I chose and definitely recommend is bringing on an associate 5-7 years before your preferred retirement date with the intention of them purchasing your practice and the selling doctor to stay on for a period as an associate to maximize financial benefits. While no plan is without challenges, this approach gives one greater control over the process. It allows the selling doctor to optimize the financial outcome but also to shape the future of their practice, align expectations with staff and patients and helps to ensure the legacy they've built to continue to grow and serve the community long after stepping away. It also provides the senior dentist an opportunity to be less stressed and able to work on their emotional and physical health in order to retire better prepared for the future. Dentistry can exact a huge physical and mental toll over time. Eighty plus percent of dentists according to the ADA Well Being Survey state they work with some degree of physical pain and hearing loss is common. Emotional and burnout cases have quadrupled in the past 20 years. Some dentists towards the end of their career tend to reduce working schedules feeling financially healthy and/or to reduce physical and mental stress but practice devaluation is the result. The idea is to maintain or increase practice value until such time as desiring to sell.

Avoid The Siren Song Of Corporate Ownership

I do not recommend selling a practice to corporate dentistry. Despite giving polished sales pitches and rosy promises, in my experience of many years, these deals rarely turn out as advertised. Corporations claim you will retain autonomy after the sale, that your only responsibility will be clinical care and that you will finally be free of the distractions of having to manage staff, handling finances or ordering supplies. In most all cases I am aware the reality is very different. What typically occurs is that control of office function shifts immediately. An office manager, the face of the corporation, steps in, imposes quotas, dictates purchasing decisions and takes over nearly every operational aspect.. In short, the selling dentist is no longer running the practice; they are under someone else's rules. What the practice resembled before the sale is often unrecognizable within a short time and you have no say so insofar as future direction. It may already be too late for some but others who still have the time and energy to plot a different path can reap the rewards of better financial outcomes and a smoother transition into retirement.

Retire On Your Own Terms

The ultimate goal is simple. Retire on your own terms when you are ready- financially, emotionally and physically healthy, ready to enjoy the next phase of life after dentistry. Ideally, when one reaches that point in life, they can walk happily or even continue working part- time purely by choice, not by necessity, avoiding the all too common scenario of being emotionally ready to retire but having to due to poor planning, bad decisions of unforeseen life events.

The Right Time For An Associate

If the practice has grown to the point where the practitioner feels overwhelmed, is turning away new patients or trying to accommodate everyone and feeling burned out all the time then it is time to call for help. Hiring an associate can relieve much pressure and support continued growth, but the question is when is the right time and what is the short and long term practice goal. Bringing in an associate can be a welcome solution but how you structure it depends a lot on the phase of career. It may be too early to consider retirement since the average dentist practices over 40 years. If you offer a buy-in/partnership at an early stage of practice life it can be fraught with potential problems because you are committing to a long, complicated personal and business relationship. Remember, business partnerships are often likened to marriages, without the intimacy, which is often the only thing that holds a marriage together. When they work, they're great. When they don't the divorce can be emotionally and financially devastating.This is not saying such situations don't work out but practice due diligence at every phase and have a contingency plan.

If early in one's career and only interested in hiring an associate who only wants a job, rather than future ownership,consider retired military or civil service dentists, clinicians seeking part-time work in order to start a family or supplement family income or others of similar genre.

Compatability Matters

In any case , evaluate the whole person beforehand. Does the candidate fit your practice culture? What are their interpersonal skills? What is their philosophy of patient care. Are they from a similar socioeconomic and geographic background as the majority of your patient base? Ivy league may find it difficult to relate to a small town, blue collar clientele . If you practice in a more rural setting someone used to urban amenities might not stay long and vice versa. The spouse matters as well. My first associate loved the outdoors, had a pickup truck and a bird dog and we interacted well but despite his happiness with the situation his wife could not adjust to small town life and it was either leave or get a divorce. That was a no brainer decision. I learned my lesson! My next associate and spouse who eventually purchased my practice loved everything about the area and the transition proceeded smoothly. Hiring a married candidate, and better with children, tends to add a bit of stability to the relationship because they are less likely to leave suddenly if you make the effort to help them feel welcome and acclimate to their new surroundings.

When considering any candidate, have your team take them to lunch since they may end up working for them. You stay away!! Your team will offer insights you may not see in a formal interview or time spent socially together. In my experience, team buy-in when considering hiring any employee often makes or breaks the long term success potential for any new hire. You want the new associate or team member to be a good fit and help rather than hurt the practice. There is nothing wrong with hiring a new graduate but do your homework first. Speak with their clinical instructors at the dental school, not just about clinical skills but also chairside manners and observed general character traits. You want to know their personality and overall mindset since you wish to have someone who can handle stress and contribute to the level you desire. Best for a new graduate with GPR or AEGD training or others capable of performing procedures you may not currently offer or wish to expand as a service. Either scenario instantly adds value to the practice and creates an income stream that helps or eliminates the time required to hand hold or subsidize their salary.

It is important to evaluate whether you have the physical space and staff to support another provider and, if not, plan for office renovations and new hires in advance as part of the growth process. It is important to have the patience and willingness to be a mentor as well because , if not, you may wish to reconsider moving forward.

Additional Benefits

Besides increasing practice income and long term practice valuation, the practice purchaser or associate is a source of support in other ways. An unbiased case second opinion is oftentimes invaluable as is the practice being covered during vacations or illness. It can relieve a lot of stress about current and future unknowns if the relationship between doctors is solid. If considering a sale within 5-7 years, having an associate allows adequate time to train, mentor and gradually and seamlessly transfer ownership and leadership responsibilities. Set the stage by allowing the associate to lead morning huddles, be involved in hiring decisions and take a visible leadership role at every opportunity. Done correctly, a transition can be done so seamlessly that, if you desire, neither staff nor patients even notice the change in ownership until you feel the time is right. In my own case, I followed this plan, sold my practice, and worked 3 years as a highly compensated associate until I announced my actual exit from the practice 6 months in advance. No one had a clue. You must obviously handle your own particular situation but you have choices. My wife and I took more time off, traveled, hired an Actuary and set up a Defined Benefit Plan and , as a single employee of my corporation, I was able to double my retirement fund in three years.

Protect Yourself

Always work with a practice transition specialist. Ideally it would be a former dentist who will have a better sense of your situation from experience. You will want to define clear roles for each dentist from the beginning, compensation methods and timeframe for subsidizing the new associates income, benefits including retirement fund, vacation and sick leave and day to day managerial responsibilities.

1. Non-compete and non solicitation clauses and patient files rights

2. Termination protocols

3. Indemnity Provisions

4. Compensation structure

5. Coverage responsibilities

6. Patient assignment expectations

7. Required CE and clinical growth

8. Duties beyond clinical work

9. Contingency planning (death, disability, exit strategies

10. Timeframes and methods for future transition and practice/real estate valuation. Do not have an open ended period for change of ownership and impede future retirement plans. At the end of the previously agreed upon period for a sale, should the associate hesitate, give them 60 days to make up their mind and, should they refuse, have the exit strategy in writing and move forward rather than being held in limbo.

There are many moving parts and hiring a good transition specialist helps insure you are legally and financially protected

Preparing For Sale

A dentist should ideally have a buy-sell agreement in place with clear timelines for the new associate before the associate even starts work if they are considered a potential practice purchaser. Once the associate proves to be a good fit and expresses interest in ownership at the previously agreed upon time period , or before if interested, start the ball rolling by hiring a good transition specialist to guide the process

A practice evaluation should have been done at the time of hiring the new associate but now it is time to put together numbers. It is best for both parties to get a separate evaluation because, if they are close, it is easier to compromise and the sale proceeds more smoothly to the satisfaction of everyone. If the valuations are far apart, hire a neutral arbitrator both parties agree on. Structure the sale to favor good will for tax benefits. Decide how accounts receivables will be handled. One clean method is for the buyer to purchase the accounts receivables in a separate contract at a fair percentage based on collections history, This provides the new buyer an instant infusion of income and simplifies future paperwork when just one party is involved. The seller may finance at some rate if desired. I recommend not financing a practice sale yourself. There is plenty of 100% financing available in most cases. Have the sale structured for the least amount of tax burden. If the seller does agree to finance they MUST demand a large upfront amount to dissuade the buyer from any unexpected forfeiture, often after running the practice into the ground. Instead, take the money up front and run and agree upon a period of swapping roles where the seller agrees to continue working full or part time as an associate at a predetermined period of time and rate of compensation. Consider a minimum of one year but preferably longer. If the seller remains as a 1099 employee they can then retain an actuary and maximize retirement funds , oftentimes doubling their previous fund value, since they are allowed to deposit larger funds as the only employee. Agreeing to continue working as an associate after the sale is a valuable asset to the buyer and can increase the initial sales price at least 10 to 15 % or more depending on the time the seller agrees to remain.

Contingency Planning

Even with the best planning, unexpected events can derail everything. Make sure the initial agreement includes the right of first refusal in case of death or disability, practice valuation scenario and protection of patient records. A term life insurance on the senior dentist, preferably paid for by the associate, with proceeds going to the spouse or estate (credited as down payment if the associate purchases the practice) is a must. This step gives the associate significant funds and better insures the sale of the practice in a timely manner.

Reflection & Practice

You have invested decades building your practice. When the time comes, make sure you, your spouse or estate are positioned to reap the full reward, not just financially, but in peace of mind and legacy. The earlier one plans the more options they have and better chances of creating a smooth, less stressful transition. Carefully evaluate your particular situation and time frame and create a future plan

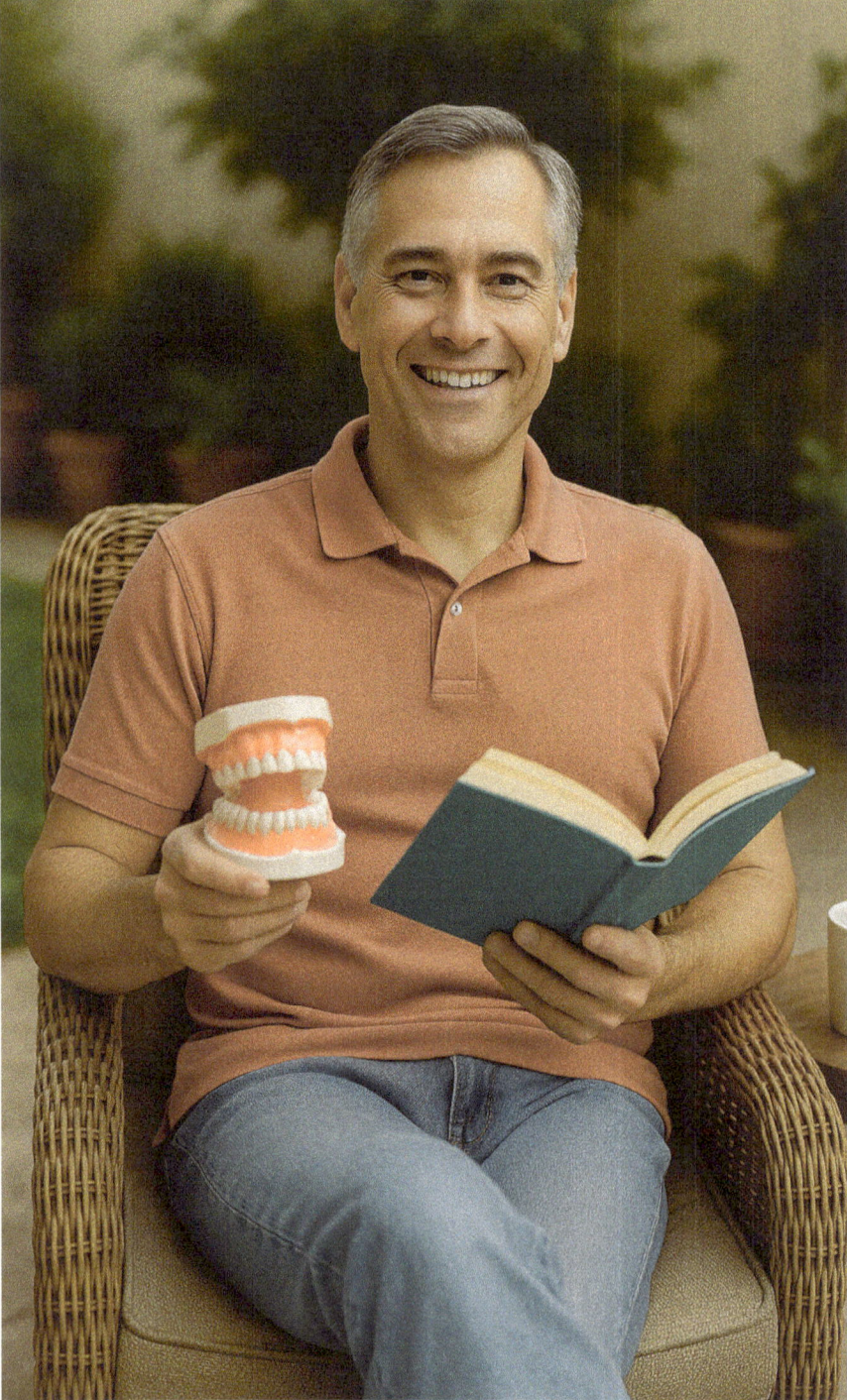

Chapter 14

Retirement Presents Opportunities To Give Back
So Much More Ahead. Yea!!!

Retirement is not an ending, but a new beginning. After decades of practice, fulfillment should not simply come from ceasing to work, but from an opportunity to redirect energy into new pursuits. The key is to never retire from having a purpose. When retiring it was with a sense of excitement for what lay ahead next. Following the concepts put forth in this book I was able to retire after 27 years financially secure and physically and emotionally healthy ready for the next chapter in life. Having led an exciting past working in construction, as a cook and dishwasher, living and working in the Bahamas, bass player in a rock band, landing on an aircraft carrier and flying numerous combat missions I knew I would not be happy with a sedentary existence. In seminars and publications over the years I have reminded people that our job should not define who we are but simply be considered a means to an end. Sadly, for many, that is not the case and upon retiring they feel lost. One should never leave one thing unless they have something to go to. Developing hobbies and outside interests, travel plans or even part time employment possibilities before retiring will result in a greater sense of worth for the future. If one desires to lessen the impact of putting up the drill a bit, volunteer and locum-tenens work is readily available..You can pick and choose your jobs and the pay is quite good because they are desperate in many cases. I work in a mobile unit several times a year and a local clinic once quarterly. PLEASE, no matter what you do, do not let your license lapse. You never know when an opportunity may arise that may be enticing. Soon after retiring I was contacted about a very lucrative, non stressful and minimally time consuming online opportunity that could be done from anywhere but required an active license. We each pursue different paths and have different interests and ambitions in this life. That is not saying one is better or worse than another, just different. People can be happy and fulfilled in numerous ways depending on likes, dislikes, personality and what they consider important in life but each of us has something later in life we can offer to benefit others.

Invaluable Experiences And Continued Self Worth

Everyone desires a continued sense of self worth and accomplishment in their later years. While working, my wife and I took very few vacations since we each had our own businesses. After retiring we began to travel more and I even attempted to play golf but that experiment ended sadly since I was a miserable failure at the sport and took up tennis instead. Over the years many people have shared the fact they were so busy in retirement they did not know how they ever had time to work which I soon discovered as well. We had no idea my dear wife would be diagnosed with incurable Parkinson's after I retired. I feel so blessed we have had extra years by retiring early to do things we could never have done 10 years later.

The opportunities to volunteer in the community became my next focus and I took full advantage. Not going into specifics, an abundance of agencies exist, so anyone sitting around bored and bemoaning their plight might investigate these opportunities since everyone has something to offer. You may be surprised at the number of local organizations in your community who need volunteer help. One source of information is the Chamber of Commerce but Google also lists non profit charitable organizations in your area. Most of us know or know of elderly, home bound or disabled individuals who are always grateful for someone to help care for their lawn, take them to lunch, provide transportation or do maintenance on or around their home or simply visit periodically. Most small churches with limited budgets need help with maintenance, committee service, yard work and maintaining cemeteries which often stand neglected. Diane and I consider our time as mentors for some Junior High students as one of our most satisfying efforts ever. Research has shown that people who volunteer have less depression, less anxiety, higher self-esteem, higher life satisfaction and a greater sense of meaning in life. Other benefits often include learning new skills, making new friends and improving one's social and relationship skills. Any way you look at it it makes us feel better about ourselves and that can't hurt.

My hope for each reader , whenever they choose to retire, is to be able to enjoy the fruits of their labor when that time comes knowing they have given so much of themselves to so many over the years and now it is their time to celebrate.

Postscript

I can truthfully say I've never been one to be jealous of another's accomplishments or success, especially those who have attained it through dedication and hard work whether they are business persons, athletes, great artists, musicians, poets or intellectuals, but I must admit it would be nice to be able to draw a straight line or play the piano. The best I can do is enjoy the beauty of their works. Despite my areas of lack, I still have been so undeservedly blessed in my life and can never complain about what I may not have done or possess. Diane and I have been so fortunate to have traveled extensively and on numerous occasions, in some museum, I will stand before a master's painting or sculpture for long periods, mesmerized. My wife tends to look and then wander and will eventually return and say, "are you still here?" The same can be said oftentimes in my reading poetry. One of my favorite poets is Edgar A. Guest, also known as the people's poet, who had an inspirational and optimistic view of everyday life and expressed it so well. His words should be guiding lights to each of us in our daily lives. I will now share two of my favorite poems. I hope you like them. Read each several times and try to absorb their meaning.

Let Me

Let me go through the day
With kindly thought for all
To live, to work, to play
And with the night recall
The journey and its care
And find no hatred there

Let me come home at night
Clear- eyed and unashamed
Still clinging to the right

My record undefamed
Let not my conscience see
The marks of shame on me.

Let me not,, mad for gain,
Or pomp or place or pride
Cause others needless pain
Or thrust the weak aside
Let no say I've been
Cruel or base or mean

Whatever may befall
My lot throughout the day
Let me come through it all
Fair as I start away.
Let me, when night brings rest
Know that I have done my best

Blessings

By the blue that bends above us,
By the smiling friends who love us,
By the laughter of a baby
And the babbling of a Brook,
By the glad Junes with their roses
And each happy day which closes
With the prayers of little children
Everywhere God turns to look,
We are blessed in countless ways
Through the number of our days.

By the hope which gilds tomorrow,
By the faith which sweetens sorrow,
By the beauty all around us
`When the dawn of day is fair,
By the health which God has lent us
For the tasks for which he sent us,
We are richly compensated
For the burdens we must bear,
And through tears of grief may fall,
God has blessed us, one and all,

By the glad smile of a neighbor,
By the joy of honest labor,
By the singing of the kettle
And the home where we may rest,
By the true friend standing by us
Through the hours when burdens try us,
By uncounted little pleasures
All our lives are richly blessed
Never year nor day nor minute,
But hold something lovely in it.

ABOUT THE AUTHOR

Dr, Gary Stough is a private practitioner in Northeast Georgia. A former Marine Corps aviator, award winning editor and past President of the GAGD, PACE CE provider and practice consultant, his focus is on attaining practice success through a combination of good clinical, leadership, business and communication skills and balancing work-personal life priorities. His focus is on attention to details, the oft neglected little things, that differentiate an average and above average practice. He is always happy to hear from readers at gstoughdmd@gmail.com

www.ingramcontent.com/pod-product-compliance
Lightning Source LLC
Chambersburg PA
CBHW071710210326
41597CB00017B/2413